# Public

# Relations

# Marketing

## Making a Splash Without Much Cash

Stephanie Seacord

**The Oasis Press®**
Central Point, Oregon

*To Richard*

Published by The Oasis Press®/PSI Research
© 1999 by Stephanie Seacord

This publication is designed to provide accurate and authoritative information in regard to the subject matter covered. It is sold with the understanding that the author and publisher are not engaged in rendering legal, accounting, or other professional service. If legal advice or other expert assistance is required, the services of a competent professional person should be sought.

> *— from a declaration of principles jointly adopted by a committee of the American Bar Association and a committee of publishers.*

Interior Design: Eliot House Productions
Cover Design: Steven Burns

Please direct any comments, questions, or suggestions regarding this book to:
    The Oasis Press®/PSI Research
    Editorial Department
    P.O. Box 3727
    Central Point, Oregon 97502-0032
    (541) 479-9464
    (541) 476-1479 fax
    *info@psi-research.com* e-mail

The Oasis Press® is a Registered Trademark of Publishing Services, Inc., an Oregon corporation doing business as PSI Research.

**Library of Congress Cataloging-in-Publication Data**
Seacord, Stephanie, 1952–
   Public relations marketing : making a splash without much cash / Stephanie Seacord.
      p. cm. – – (PSI successful business library)
   Includes index.
   ISBN: 1-55571-459-5 (paper)
    1. Public relations. 2. Marketing. 3. Advertising. I. Title.
II. Series.
HD59.S36   1999
659.2 – –dc21                        99–18207
                                      CIP

Printed and bound in the United States of America

First Edition 10 9 8 7 6 5 4 3 2 1

 Printed on recycled paper when available

# Table of Contents

# Acknowledgments

To acknowledge those who contributed to the creation of this book, I can thank those who have shaped my career in public relations marketing over the past 25 years, starting with Ferne Arfin and Jesse Mohorovic who hired me as part-time junior account executive at Ingalls PR. They taught me the craft, from writing with a typewriter to creating an annual report.

Considerable thanks go to those colleagues who sometimes became clients, and often became friends, in particular Sheila Schofield. The legacy of Omni-Dunfey Hotels will long endure with people including Sheila, Paul Sacco, Jon Crellin, Lesley Livingston-Silberstein, Mary Carella, Philip Georgas, and the PR Task Force: Joanne Fine, Sheila King, Mary Tamposi, and Aimee Noonan. In the course of experiencing life on both sides of the agency-client contract I find other voices have added their thoughts here: Rea Lubar, Sally Jackson, Joyce Martin, Patrice Tanaka, Vicki Feldman, Alicia Baker, Lou Trubiano and Irma Mann, among them. Yes, Gary Leopold, it is a "good gig;" and no — nameless others — I shouldn't have "chosen another field." To editors and reporters including: Bill Gillette, Phil Hayward, Ed Watkins, Kristen O'Meara, Katrina Brown, Rick Eyerdam, Charlie Sherman, Jerry Morris, Dave Rodman, you continue to be great customers.

It's always a delight when you take my call. To clients including Ben Cammarata of TJX; Dick Devlin of *Sail* Magazine; Rosemary Waugh of Acorn Structures; Bill Begley of Microtel; and John Wall of B. Wall Motorventures, I owe many important lessons. Obviously you knew what you were doing. In fact, I thank John Wall, Ernie Saxton, and Chris Economacki — who placed a little notice in his paper that I would be writing the columns from which this book originated in Ernie Saxton's *Motorsports Marketing News*. That prompted John to call and inquire whether I would be available to help market his new Busch North race team and driver, Bryan Wall — for opening the door into a world that is definitely not Kansas. To my much-loved mother and sisters, thanks for honing my appreciation of different viewpoints. Finally, thank you again to my best editor, Richard; to my publisher Emmett Ramey on the West Coast, and the editor of this book, Karen Billipp, on the East, for bringing these words into focus.

# Introduction

## *The Basics of Public Relations Marketing*

In old-style vernacular, a PR person was known as a "flack." In many circles (politics comes to mind) PR people are still put in the position of having to be flacks. The difference is looking at PR as a strategic, results-oriented, cost-effective marketing tool, instead of publicity. PR marketing is an approach that cares very much whether the positioning is good or bad while publicity PR goes by the mantra, "any ink is good ink." Those of us who have not only the choice but the responsibility to be something else, something better, can achieve the results we seek by following a few Public Relations Marketing Basics which form the substance of this book. To give you an idea of where we're going, here are the concepts:

1. *Be prepared.* It's what you're paid to do. Know your deadlines (event dates, writers' schedules, editorial calendars and lead times) and ready your information (press releases, pitch letters) so you're in the starting block when the gun goes. It's hard enough to win the race without starting from behind and with enough other competitors who will try to get there before you do. Why penalize yourself?

2. *Find the real news hook — instead of fluff — in the stories you sell.* Believe it or not, editors and reporters don't like to say "no." Their job is to find the story, not shut the door in your face. It takes look-

ing at it from their point of view to figure out what's news to them. Honestly, if something is news to you, it will be news to a reporter. In fact most times something's news to you, you have to figure out a way not to tell anyone else before it's "official." Since your job is saying something "for the record" — either to keep the business' name in front of your audience or to keep premature rumors from leaking — it is critical that your media relations be the work of a professional: prepared, factual, timely, and reflective of your understanding that reporters are people, too. If a reporter has a choice between someone who's always complaining that s/he didn't use their press release (probably because there was nothing in it s/he could use) or didn't talk about his or her client, and someone who can be depended upon to provide good information and to follow up promptly if more information is needed, which call do you think that reporter will take — or make?

3. *Demonstrate that PR people are strategic marketers and craftsmen, not flacks.* Too often, PR gets a black eye because its practitioners are inexperienced. The most junior person is often assigned to the task of writing press releases even though this function is actually the formal presentation of your client's image to the world. In the most successful client-agency relationships, success is the result of real-time partnerships because strategy and tactics are nearly indistinguishable in today's marketing arena. The window of marketing opportunity has been narrowed because of the speed of communications, especially the Internet. PR work is done most effectively by professionals who can think on their feet and respond much more quickly to opportunities than ever before. Your goal as a PR person must be to recognize opportunities to tell your client's story when and where they present themselves — and to write/package the story in the most compelling way you can in order to capitalize on that opportunity to the fullest. Ultimately, achieving this goal requires creative self-discipline. Take the time and care to make that first sentence grab the reader.

4. *Take the time to stay organized.* You don't want to carry the bags of a PR person. They're full of paper. So are their offices. All of us keep all sorts of clippings and leads we've read as well as being the official records-keeper and historian for our clients. On top of these resources (sometimes literally) we must keep media lists, press kits and releases, clips and clip analyses and a variety of trade information. In our computers you'll find releases, reports, and databases, as well as e-mail addresses and Internet bookmarks. (The

computer guy in our office was amazed I had so many e-mail addresses in my personal address book and was even more amazed to find out that all of them were business-related: editors, free-lancers, series directors.) The more organized and up-to-date you keep all of this information, the more effective you will be. And the better able you'll be to get help when you need it, such as when you're on the road, because you'll be able to tell someone back in the office where to find that critical piece of information you need.

5. *Check and recheck.* How many times have you spotted the typo when you're standing at the copy machine in the middle of making 100 press kits. Don't depend on your computer spell-check, either. It doesn't differentiate between "two" and "tow." Both are real word. If you're prepared and organized, you'll even have the time to leave whatever you've written for a couple of hours and then reread your copy for content as well as accuracy. And check your facts — including the names and addresses of the people on your mailing list.

6. *Keep it simple.* Although we're advancing the cause of the PR person as strategic marketer and great writer, some of the best writing is short. Use the simple word, the familiar expression instead of a high falutin' one. Just use proper grammar. When you take the second look at your copy, make liberal use of the "delete" key. Use the best word instead of many, perambulating ones. Learn to tie the correct knot, instead of a tangle of knots.

7. *Remember that what your audience wants is the information.* A reporter doesn't care about a fancy (expensive) press kit cover with lots of cute die-cuts and foil stamping. If the design makes the information hard to get at, they will care enough to send it to the nearest waste-basket. Join the PR professionals' battle to convince art directors that form *must* follow function.

8. *Keep up on your reading.* To be an information officer for your client, you must be aware of how his or her business fits in the grander scheme of things. To find the news hook on which to hang your story, you must know what the trends are. And to put your client out in front, you need to apply the best practices which have worked for others, as well as innovations of your own. The best way to find out all of this context, as well as to keep your own mind and imagina-tion in gear is to read: your industry trades, Internet sites, and the major daily and business newspaper(s) and magazines you hope to work for your client's behalf.

9. *Make your sales contacts stand out.* When you mail a press release, the recipients should see your envelope as one containing interesting, accurate information. Using letterhead — especially a bright (but legible) background color, and some type of notice on the outside of the envelope (a colorful sticker, a dated-material stamp) can make a difference in whether your release gets opened. When it comes to e-mail, think simple and direct. Get to the point. Cut and paste your release — and then edit it — instead of attaching a file. The same is true of your phone contacts. Get to the point — but it's okay to take a few minutes to cultivate your relationship. Just be genuine. Create an identity. Don't let yourself be mistaken for one of those telemarketers who start every cold call with, "How are you?"

10. *A corollary: Have a life!* The best PR people are those with generalized backgrounds or liberal arts degrees. You don't need to go to technical school or get a journalism degree to be a great PR professional. You need to understand how the world works: why people keep doing the same things; what makes cultures distinctive; what people care about. Once you start working, why would you stop looking around? If you can't justify an hour on a bench in the sunshine, or two hours walking down a country lane, tell yourself it's research. You won't feel so guilty — and you'll probably discover some new idea that's been lurking around in the cobwebs too unformed to be noticed until you cleared the cobwebs away. You think the guys who invented Yahoo! and are now worth the net value of Boeing worry about whether they're the first ones in and the last to leave the office every day? Do you think they even have offices to go to?

Public Relations is the craft of managing information. It's not about deception, although there are some extremely successful PR executives who have understood "management" to be "manipulation." It's not about ego; it's about competition and making your enterprise more successful, more appreciated by its customer audience than your competition. (Of course, both your ego and your client's must be strong enough to stand up to the media challenge.) The successful public relations campaign makes what you're saying memorable; and that's your ultimate goal: make your message stand out enough that people do what you'd like them to do — buy your product or service, sponsor your activity, support your position.

# Making a Splash Without Much Cash

There are some companies that just seem bigger than life. You see them everywhere. You see their logos in the most unlikely places. They're the ones who seem to coup the best opportunities. They are the companies that seem to have come out of nowhere and onto center stage in the American consciousness.

These are the companies that are generally quite large by the time they seem to be everywhere; but the entrepreneur who looks for answers to the "how did they do it?" question quickly discovers parallels and similarities with his or her own experience. The secret to these companies' success is, inevitably, marketing — especially the sort of PR-on-a-shoestring budget that this book explores.

Consider these once-small companies:

- Top of the Tree Baking Company, a northeast regional pie company that now distributes to most of the major supermarket chains in New England. Not that long ago Top of the Tree sold 2,700 apple pies in two minutes on the Home Shopping Network. How did the company become so successful? The main reason is that Gordon "Pie"berger (aka Weinberger), the president of Top of the Tree Baking Company, is a PR wizard. He used to work for one of the big consumer product agencies; then one day he decided to take his grandmother's apple pie recipe to the street. He believed so strongly in the power of PR that he spent not one nickel on advertising his new product during the first years of start-up.

- Another example: the smart marketers of the start-up snack company, Smart Food, hired a prop plane to scatter bags of their product (that they were still sealing themselves with a hand-driven machine) over a crowded summer beach. This "splash" made more sense to them than spending money on other marketing media.

- Splashdown USA, gave jackets away to such high profile boaters as Dennis Conner, Chris Dickson, and Wally Schirra (the astronaut, whose powerboat is, fittingly, named Splashdown). They also gave jackets to the winners of sailing regattas in such markets as Marblehead, Newport, Noroton, Long Beach, Grosse Pointe, and Manhattan. This was their way to build awareness for the brand among Splashdown's key customer groups.

In the clamorous environment of modern society and its multiple media, you have to make a splash for anyone to even notice — particularly if you are a small company. Smart PR marketers are not born, nor are they found only in mega brand companies like Coca-Cola and Ford. They are people who look for strategic opportunities to make a visible impression on the right audience, who understand the basic principles of PR, and who use the basic, tried and true tools of professional public relations. Making a splash does not require lots of cash. Like Gordon Pieberger, you should set the goal of never paying for anything until all the other avenues have been exhausted for making an audience aware of your message for free.

When you think of PR, think of making a statement, making noise in order to get attention. Then remember that once you have people's attention, you must have something important to say to the audience you've attracted. The idea is to make people — preferably that select group of people identified as the ones who shouldn't be able to live without the product or service in question — sit up and take notice of what you're saying.

The trick is, there can be no trick. The days of blue smoke and mirrors, dirty deeds, and "all form and no substance" are gone. Consumers may be cynical but they're not stupid. Every survey of buying habits reports that customers choose products based on the total image they have of a company — and support companies who take an interest in the same issues they hold dear. NASCAR fans are fanatically loyal to those companies, large and small, who support the sport by sponsoring the teams and races.

Because consumers have learned that by being an educated consumer they come out ahead, they read up on "how to do it right" for every subject they encounter. Then you decide to drop a new idea into their awareness pool, such as news about a product or service never offered before. But your target is not a smooth pond. The commercial environment looks more like the surf tossed up by a Force Four gale. Success depends on making waves or, at least, on riding the crests of the ones that have already formed in the public's mind.

Believe it or not, this is not difficult to do. Challenging, yes. Frustrating, tiring, seemingly endless, and as draining as performing on stage, but not difficult. The secret is:

- Identify the audience.
- Deliver the message.
- Supply a reason to "get it."
- Provide easy access for the purchase — literally as well as figuratively moving any barriers that stand in the way.

So, everyone from Xerox to Mary Kay says the same thing. The process of selling is a matter of understanding needs, overcoming objections, translating features into benefits, and closing the sale. The problem is filling the house to watch the tap dance.

The most effective public relations marketing efforts in memory have a few things in common:

- They were short-term, high impact bursts that cut through the clutter.
- They were hip, meaning timely, strokes of genius that captured a well-known moment and rode the wave. Gordon "Pieberger" staged a photo op during the last campaign with his American apple pie and the Presidential candidates when they toured his Manchester plant before the New Hampshire primary.
- They were smart — they made the audience grab hold of the concept.
- They (sometimes) cared and made you care. (Thank you, American Airlines "up where the sun is always shining and the sky is always blue.")

Orchestrate all of these elements, use professional knowledge to get to the media (and customers) when and wherever they'll be receptive to the pitch. Then deliver on the promise of quality, and success will follow.

How can you accomplish all this nirvana without much cash? Pick the investments wisely.

## If Image Is So Important, Make the Visual Identity Sparkle

This is a matter of good design, not expensive printing. Look at the logotypes and corporate identities for the companies who spend literally billions of dollars on collateral. A hotel company I worked with decided that in order to attract a new investor, it needed a Madison Avenue logo. Several hundred thousand dollars later, it had one: a stylized, two-color design that conveyed "sophisticated warmth and soft hospitality" — or words to that effect. The Florida Tourism Commission reportedly spent $350,000 redesigning its logo and Website identity to the colorful FLAUSA. Alternatively, the no-money-invested Splashdown logo, a simple red, blue, and yellow square, tipped on end, made a big splash with no such outlay and had the following advantages:

- A shape that was so simple and yet so different from the competitors' "name" brands, it could be recognized from halfway across Earl's Court at the London Boat Show.

- The basic primary colors of red, blue, and yellow made it easy to reproduce — no fancy PMS colors that can be difficult to match, or difficult to reproduce when printed on colored stocks. Plus, when printed two-color (red and blue) on yellow paper, the same effect resulted, without paying for a third ink color.

- The name itself, "Splashdown" was part of the design, lending it a definitely contemporary, partly high-tech feel. Everybody in England thought it was an American company, since the word was popularized with the U.S. space program.

## Packaging Is as Important for a Communications Program as It Is for a Product

Editors say a professional-looking envelope, with a direct-printed address rather than a label, is much more likely to be opened than one that isn't. They say using letterhead and being a stickler for clean, grammatical copy adds credibility to what's being said. Color stands out. You wouldn't expect to get four times the pick-up for a St. Patrick's Day press release with little foil shamrocks on the envelope. But that was the case when compared to the response for the same event the previous year.

Remember that the editors who get press releases, and the customers who get newsletters or brochures are being buried in direct marketing materials at the rate of thousands of pieces per American per year. Give them a reason to open it. Or don't make them have to open it at all — postcards are great, and cost two-thirds of the postage of envelopes.

Think in three-dimensions. Like the mailer on performance shocks that suspension shop, Leading Edge Motorsport, had done. At the start of the racing season in April, they put a "Junior Slinky" (the metal one, not the plastic) in a small box with a brochure and an insert printed out on company letterhead that said "SPRING! No, not the season, the suspension component" and mailed it to all the race shops in the area. Total cost: about $35. The first referral was for a $300 job.

## Invest Sweat-Equity

PR Marketing demands that you keep the *product* in front of the target audience at every opportunity. Not only does this provide sales pitch and networking opportunities, it's an opportunity to respond to whatever comes up, especially chances to donate product or solve a problem in a high-profile, highly-appreciated environment.

Lean operations stuff their boxes and press kits themselves; and learn how to run the software and office machines for slick-looking proposals. They put customizing stickers on catalogs while they're watching TV. They think, "How can I do this faster and better myself?" Then they find the ways.

Every "roots in the garage and grab hold of a star" case study talks about these things — and about the moments of despair. "Ma" Gertsner, CEO of then-startup Columbia Sportswear, determined to keep the company her late husband had founded the day her lawyer sat at her kitchen table and tried to fleece her out of it. She said, "How would you like it if someone tried to screw your widow the way you're screwing me?" Then she fired him, went on to make millions in sales, and become one of the hottest outfitters in the nation. Notice whose jackets The Weather Channel people are wearing if you want to see smart PR marketing and brilliant product positioning at work.

PR is the art of persuasion. Yes, certainly, if you shove somebody's hat on the winner's head, the fans can't help noticing what the brand is. But if Jeff Gordon drinks his sponsor's soda, after a long, hot, thirsty race, the fan may reach for his own Pepsi. When Jeff Gordon takes a long slug of Pepsi at the Coca Cola 500, he fires another broadside in the ongoing cola wars — and that's what guerrilla marketing is all about. It ain't pretty, but it's effective.

On a kinder, gentler plane, take the example of the traveling Sparky. Last season, a group of fifth graders sent a stuffed dog on a marathon with the Petty NASCAR race team — a great way for kids to learn some geography. Also a great way for Petty Enterprises to earn goodwill among race fans, as it was their prescient PR person who sent out the press release, photo and caption that got picked up in all the trades. Ask yourself why Petty Enterprises would bother. Then remember that Petty Enterprises is a business — just like yours. Whenever they have a chance to get a positive association (and what could be more positive than a stuffed animal, adopted as a mascot?) in front of their fans, they earn a bigger share of the market, at least for the moment. Set aside whether or not the team sold more T-shirts as a result of the "warm fuzzies" they created in their audience with the story. They earned: 1) more awareness; and 2) goodwill. As anyone involved in the motorsports marketing phenomenon of NASCAR will tell you, goodwill from a NASCAR fan is precursor to sales, more so in NASCAR than any other major league sport.

So, PR is the art of persuading your audience to: 1) be aware of you; and 2) form positive associations with your name.

Awareness is an interesting concept, one that is measured to the tenth of a percent in America. A sports marketing client in England never understood why we kept giving product away at major events. They said, "In the 15 years we've been in business, we've never given anything away." They just didn't get it, in spite of telling them that, in America — where they were trying to establish a market — if a potential customer says, "I've never heard of you," it doesn't matter how good your product is.

Think about it. How many times have you winced when a customer or sponsor said, "Never heard of it" when you tried to make a pitch? Hearing about it, seeing it, catching a glimpse of it in some celebrity's hand — that's what building awareness is all about.

One of the key roles of public relations, therefore, is to recognize and/or create opportunities to build awareness. If you want to get technical about it you can conduct pre- and post-action surveys to measure how well your initiatives are working. In the case of the English company, their brand had a .01 awareness rating among their key audience, so there was a long way to go. Getting their product on the backs of some of the best athletes in the sport was a good way to get the product in front of their potential customers.

For a team sponsor, opportunities for building awareness include putting the sponsor's name on everything from the car to the hauler to the contingent of employees in the stands. It also means awarding product where you can. Building awareness depends on repetition of the association between your product or service and your involvement in whatever niche you may have decided to sponsor. In these media-happy days of cable television, specialized newsletters, and the Internet, a PR person could be occupied full-time just getting new messages out to all the relevant media.

## *Positive Associations*

Positive association is the second step on our philosophical journey through the practice of PR marketing.

People are motivated by impressions they store in the backs of their heads. The cognitive information comes through their senses, tumbles around as it's being sorted into the categories of previously-stored information and opinion, and flashes on some internal screen whenever the guy in the person-suit (the average consumer) realizes he needs lunch or a new battery for the Chevy. According to the experts, information in the form of advertising gets stirred around in the sorter a bit longer, because the recipient of the message knows that the information is biased — it's only what the advertiser wants to tell him about the burger or battery — and it's hard to know whether to believe the claims. Recent studies have found that the endorsement-style ad (especially the celebrity endorsement) is growing less and less effective because people understand that the endorser is being paid to make the claim.

Publicity — an article or mention of your product, service, or team by a reporter — goes into the "believable information" files, and goes there more directly. If the audience believes the source — either because a reporter has a reputation for accuracy or inside information, or because the publication or broadcast program lends the same credibility to all the people who write or report for it — the information tends to go straight to the back of the head, as if the reader or listener had done all the investigation and conclusion-drawing him or herself. That's why publicity is such an important tool in persuading people to do what you want.

Interestingly enough, thanks to all the images Americans are bombarded with on a daily basis, the really savvy advertisers are now delivering totally bizarre messages and pictures to sell their products (frogs and lizards to sell Budweiser, for example), so that the product name goes straight to that "hind brain" and is served up as "top of the mind awareness" when a choice has to be made about what brand of beer to buy. The message never gets sorted (it can't be!). It's either a positive association with Budweiser — you think Louie the Lizard should have his day — or you think the whole thing is dumb.

Your two goals in producing effective public relations, have to be getting your world to pay attention, and then saying something that motivates the audience to do what you want.

All the tools, like qualified media lists and editorial calendars, complete and accurate press kits, timely press releases, special events, media relations, and photo opportunities (even stuffed dogs), are means to those ends, *not* the other way around.

Having Sparky in the race car doesn't do anything. Sending a picture of Sparky — the only stuffed dog on the Winston Cup circuit — to the newspapers, separates you from the rest of the pack, and creates a feeling that goes straight to the hind brains of your fans.

That is what "warm fuzzies" are all about.

## *Looking Down from the Blimp*

A good analogy comes from a description a colleague offered about his friend, the chairman of HFS Corp., the company that encompasses franchising rights to nine hotel brands (including Howard Johnson and Super 8), three home real estate brokerage firms (Century 21, ERA, and Coldwell Banker), Avis, International Resorts timeshare, and PHH, a company that handles executive relocations, fleet vehicle rentals, and mortgage origination. In describing why, the company and their CEO had been so phenomenally successful, this admirer said, "Other people look down from the stadium; Henry (Silverman, the CEO) looks down from the blimp."

The idea of PR marketing is to be smart enough to look down from the blimp. The patterns that emerge (like a company that controls franchising services for hotels, rental car, timeshares, and home purchasing) are so clear you wonder why no one noticed them before.

In the interest of promoting the view from the blimp, take a look at some of the big picture commitments you should be thinking of as you map out your marketing strategy.

## Have You Focused, Yet?

Do you know what your goal is for the year? Will you recognize opportunities to advance that goal through promotions, marketing communications, and special events when they come along? If your goal is to improve marketshare, what will you do differently than last year to avoid the mistakes you made then? If your goal is to improve your brand awareness, how will you ensure that you earn more recognition from the folks who decide where their dollars go? If your goal is to increase revenues, is your marketing plan just a gleam in someone's eye, or is it kicking butt and taking names already?

Not one of these goals will be achieved if you don't define them and the steps necessary to get there. Set objectives, and stay on track. Send out press releases on a regular schedule; create that newsletter for your customer database.

## Do You Understand What Your Objectives Are?

Look at the example of motorsports marketing. If you think race car sponsors all look for a big logo on the race car, ask yourself why Burger King switched from a four-foot hood-covering logo to a presence not much bigger than a Whopper on Dale Earnhardt's right shoulder. Or what about HFS's Super 8 brand? Super 8 Director of Motorsports Marketing, Tom McNulty is the first to say you'll only see their logo when the race car's parked in the pits. What he wants out of motorsports marketing is the chance to "move the barricades" for key customers. He wants to give his best customers, his most effective salespeople, and the travel agents who help him sell Super 8 rooms a chance to rub elbows with the stars of the sport. By associating with a Winston Cup team, Super 8 gains that entrée. The security people will literally move the barricades that cordon off parking and hospitality areas reserved for sponsor events. The same is (or should be true) for any sponsor of any special event (or medium).

David Wible at Red Roof derived more benefit from introducing driver Patty Moise to travel agents who book Red Roof stays than he did from the television exposure for the logo. There are many, many sponsors who tag onto the back of a race car because of the customer, employee, and vendor relations opportunities motorsports provides. How will you help your business, client, or sponsor achieve similar goals?

## How Will You Make a Splash This Year?

It's not enough to be good, you have to tell people how and why you're better than your competition; and you have to be creative — and credible — in the way you go about making your impression.

A motorsports business might conclude that to make a big splash, you could go build yourself a blimp and then offer it for Speedvision or ESPN as a camera platform. But if you did that, would you have any money left to build your cars?

So how do you decide where your promotional dollars should go? In management circles, they call it "thinking outside the box," which is another way of saying, "take a look down from the blimp." What would make an impression on you, on your spouse, on the friends and customers of your company?

If other companies are giving away hats for a promo, maybe you want to give away mini-umbrellas. But if you don't have hats, will people keep saying, "why don't you guys have hats?" It's about expectations. Just keep the whole scene in perspective in your pursuit of the big impression. If someone had suggested hats and sunscreen for the First Annual Bahamas Vintage Car Festival, they would have been disappointed with the actual weather — it rained much of the weekend. Then again, the top of Sterling Moss' head would have appreciated the decision to go ahead with the sunscreen.

## How Will You "Move the Barricades" for the People Very Important to Your Goals?

Why do so many PR people take the care and feeding of their clients and sponsors so casually? Time and again there are sponsors who abandon a series or a team because no one has time to talk to them, companies who are getting an incredible bargain but perceive no value in it because the team isn't taking the time to translate the features into benefits and return on investment.

It takes a very sophisticated marketing mind to see value in a commitment if the sponsor's representative has a lousy time when he or she comes to the event. If you are anxious to "palm off" the sponsor on the PR people, perhaps you should take a long hard look at your business ethics from the blimp … and in the mirror.

## One More "Real World" Caution

The best lesson of all in making a splash without much cash is to stay smart, and ahead of the competition. If living well is the best revenge, then knowing a competitor spent hundreds of times the money you spent to recreate your marketing event, is sweet. Just remember the Golden Rule: He who has the gold, rules. So stay up on your game. Be a PR marketer, not just a publicist. Some of the experiences and suggestions in this book may help.

# Company Brochures

Effectively using PR requires that you have a full toolbox — a "quiver of arrows" as my Manhattan PR colleague Rea Lubar put it in her award-winning capabilities brochure. Tools like capabilities brochures and press releases allow you to follow up professionally, effectively, and efficiently after you've achieved the first mission of getting your audience's attention.

Each of these basic tools will be explored in individual chapters, starting with the company brochure. Every business — even those who have Websites — should have a brochure that clearly describes what product or service you offer your customers.

Many companies distribute glossy, four-color catalogs, that enticingly and appropriately present their product range. But for those with limited budgets, it's especially important to have a core piece you can leave with a prospective customer. There are so many opportunities to hand out a brochure, something more than a business card. The minimal investment you make in time and cost to produce a brochure can yield a high return.

## The Purpose of a Brochure

The primary purpose of a brochure is to tell people who and what your business does. The cover should feature the company name, address and phone, including 800 number, fax, e-mail, and Website address. The language should be simple, and the thoughts expressed concisely. *USA Today* now writes for the comprehension level of a sixth grader. No matter how sophisticated the audience, the best rule for writing is, keep it simple.

The second purpose of the brochure is to position the business in the minds of potential customers as a reliable provider of the product or service detailed in the brochure.

You might argue that it's easier to tell people about the business in person, that personal, face-to-face communication is better. That may be, but some of the other people in the company may not be as effective communicators. What about all those people you never see face to face? What of the people who call for information, and the people your assistants talk to. Will those employees remember to talk about all the special details and key phrases you've accumulated over the years of building the business?

The chief benefit of a brochure is that it frames the story precisely, wherever the mail or a trade show or a pass-along happens to take it. A brochure is an "instant best salesperson" — on his or her best day, in the most positive frame of mind and at their most logical and eloquent. In fact, a brochure can say things about the business' quality and track record that you might be too modest to say yourself.

The company brochure should be the first image-producing step you take after printing your business cards. Why? Because this is an information society, an increasingly anonymous, data-gathering society. People are afraid to ask questions for fear of looking dumb — or being lied to by overzealous salespersons who will harass them if they aren't ready to buy. The brochure is your greatest prospecting ally. It can educate consumers and develop idle curiosity into sales potential. If you can hit their hot buttons, consumers who didn't even know they needed the product or service will become customers. This is especially true of small companies on the materials or technology frontier. A brochure is one more finishing touch, that projects professionalism for the outfit.

## Production

When it comes to producing the brochure, a few tips will help get the most from the investment.

**Size.** The brochure needs to be flexible and inexpensive to get the maximum use out of it. The size should therefore make the brochure easy to produce, with no odd-sized, expensive paper sizes, folds or cuts. The standard paper sizes for printers are 8½" x 11", 11" x 14" and 11" x 17". A three or four-panel single sheet, folded to 3" x 8½" meets these paper standards and fits easily in a business-sized envelope or jacket pocket. For the higher-ticket product audience, a bound 8½" x 11" brochure works well. Even with a color-copied cover and wire spiral binding, you have an inexpensive but impressive piece.

In the hotel industry, the brochure standard is the rack card: a 3" x 8" color card that gives pertinent details about the hotel and its size along with a map and directions on how to get there. The rack card is especially effective for display in those tourist information racks the Visitors' Bureau maintains at highway rest stops. Race teams use driver cards; performers and models use head sheets. The goal is for form to *follow* function.

**Colors.** Adding some color to the brochure adds excitement and professionalism — without adding much cost. The graphics in the brochure should reflect the image of the company, and reinforce the impact of the logo. Picking an accent color for that logo, and repeating it in the brochure completes the impression. Your local quick-print shop can do a two-color job in a matter of days. Pick black for the text (it's the easiest to read), and the second color for headlines and/or design elements. Think about a colored paper (it's little extra cost); but make sure to keep the text readable. A note of caution: remember the consequences of mixing colors. Red ink on yellow paper produces orange text, unless the shade of red is carefully chosen to balance out the extra yellow of the sheet.

**Paper.** When you talk about paper, the printer will ask what weight stock to use. Letter-weight and quality (about a 60 pound text sheet) is fine for a brochure. It takes ink well, does not show through and folds with a nice crisp edge. Lighter stock can leave dark areas on the back of photos or other heavily-inked sections — and gives a flimsier impression. Heavier stock simply adds cost for the printing and for postage. A three-panel 8½" x 11" sheet, can be mailed without an envelope for the cost of a letter.

**Type.** The quality and availability of personal computers has revolutionized the typesetting process, making everyone a part-time publisher. The benefit to this is that you can produce professional-looking brochures, letters, and proposals. You can even customize each piece and have it look as if a typesetter prepared it.

The drawback is that most people don't have the expertise and experience of someone who makes a living as a typesetter. Two problems result: 1) you are tempted to print from a none-too-clear original (rather than from a printer's-black mechanical); and 2) you are tempted to use every type-style the computer can create in the same single page of text. The circus-flyer approach to brochure design is the mark of an amateur; but worse, it gets in the way of the reader's ability to follow the message.

The brochure should be designed to sell the product or service. If it's not approachable, understandable, and physically easy to read, the brochure is not meeting the objective it was intended to answer.

Therefore, pick *one* typeface, preferably a "serif" face that looks like book type (Times Roman is the most popular). Upper and lower case, please, even for the headlines. Text set in all-capital letters is hard to read. Use bold and italic versions of that face if necessary. The headline type can be different to change the mood — a sans-serif headline type is okay because there aren't a lot of words for the reader to stumble over. Make the sentences short — no more than nine words. That's the limit for billboards — it's what readers grasp as they breeze by. Break up the paragraphs with sub-heads or mini-headlines, which are also an interesting place to use the second color.

Look at those three- and four-page letters asking for a contribution or dona-tion. The message is highlighted, so that all you have to do is read the underlined parts to get a complete picture of what they have to say. Use the same approach in your brochure. Like those letters, don't be afraid to put in enough information to satisfy the person who is really interested in what your company has to say. As long as the key points are highlighted for an easy read, the details (statistics, examples, testimonials) will add credibility and further convince the customer who's leaning in your direction.

One further note about the actual typesetting. Most printers are happy to take the text on disk or receive e-mailed text. They usually ask you to save what was written as an ASCII or Text Only file, that is the universal language of computers, no matter what software is used. The quality of the output is optimized, because the type goes directly from memory to production, without any deterioration from copying. Give the printer a layout as well as scanned or camera-ready art for logos, graphics, and photos.

**Copy.** One of the most effective approaches for presenting information is the question and answer format. Answer the questions most customers ask — and those you wish they'd ask. Set up the flow in logical steps. For example:

Q: Why is PR an important marketing tool?

Q: Isn't PR the same as advertising?

Q: Why choose my company?

Q: What are the priorities and why?

Q: What should I expect as a result of a PR program?

Q: How long will it take and how much will it cost?

Notice how each question has its own space and how the "Q" acts as a bullet to itemize each thought. It's an easy-to-skim, easy-to-follow format.

Decide what are the most common questions prospective customers ask are; then answer them in a manner that is both honest and positive. If the product or service is expensive, explain why and what the benefits are. It's much easier to discuss costs and payment plans in print than in person, so the potential customer isn't embarrassed to find out the price is out of his league. The brochure detailing a high-cost item or service must also clearly define the price-value relationship, so the customer who thinks your product or service is expensive has the facts. That way, the customer doesn't shy away from talking about his or her needs, operating under the misguided impression that your company won't do what s/he wants or can afford.

As all the sales courses explain, selling is a matter of translating the features of the product or service into benefits that answer the needs of the customer. The goal is to have customers recognize that what they need is what you can provide. Make sure to define that what your operation provides is better than someone else's.

The brochure should supply answers and make the customer want to respond. A call to action — a special offer extended to all new customers such as a free consultation, or a coupon for 10 percent off, or a prominent reminder of the toll-free 800 number or Website — is the type of nudge to get your prospect to react.

## Summary

To recap, a brochure is as essential as a business card because it works as a sales ambassador. Once a brochure exists you will find lots of ways to use it: to mail to a new member list you've just acquired, to hand out at trade shows, speaking engagements, and special events, to leave on sales calls, and to include in proposals.

Don't forget to put some in the glove box and at the reception desk, and give them to relatives and friends. Aside from finally explaining to your mother what you do, you never know what potential client she might encounter!

## *Brochure Checklist*

**Size:** ❑ Does it fit in a #10 envelope?

**Color:** ❑ Four-color printing is not necessary. Two colors are plenty.
❑ Use the same color(s) as the logo to reinforce the image.

**Paper:** ❑ Is there a colored paper that will add impact?
❑ What's the weight? 60-65 pound stock is fine for a self-mailer brochure (i.e., no envelope needed.)

**Type:** ❑ Is the type a serif type, at least 12 pt. in size, with enough space ("leading") between the lines to be easy to read?
❑ How many different type styles are used? More than three (including headlines) is too many.

**Text:** ❑ Is the copy written in simple, not condescending, easy-to-understand language?
❑ Is the text divided with sub-heads and graphics?
❑ Are the most important points highlighted?
❑ Are the full name of the business, the address and phone/fax/800 number/e-mail and Website address included, in a place that's easy to reference?

# CHAPTER 3

# *Customer Databases:*
# Who's Been Sleeping in My Bed?

The most basic question when it comes to PR marketing is: "Who is my customer?" The more specific you can be in answering this question, the easier it will be to find and sell to that key customer. Airline and hotel frequent traveler programs were started on this premise. In exchange for some demographic and preference data, customers received free travel. The beauty of the system was being able to market directly to people who were known customers. The beauty of the system today is being able to focus a small budget on exactly the customer you most want to reach. It's a highly effective, low-cost PR marketing "splash."

Everybody likes walk-ins; but only someone like McDonald's can live on them. There are only a few lucky companies selling products or services who have the broad general appeal of McDonald's. The point is you need to define and describe the customer in order to go hunting for him or her in the right places and at the right times. Why does this matter?

It matters because the secret in marketing is getting the okay from your niche audience to continue a dialogue. You start by simply asking, "Are you interested in knowing more about us?" Even a traditional program using your own customer information is more effective than finding new prospects to talk to.

Just as there are six different kinds of Kleenex®, to answer the needs of pocket-pack, junior, man-sized, regular, and boutique users, there are magazines, clubs, and affinity groups for virtually every type of interest, from self-employed professionals to automotive interior hardware manufacturers. All of these people are accustomed to having you cater to their specific needs.

For example, in the hotel business, even if you're a 10-room inn, the first division of customers is into either the leisure group or the business travel group. It's pretty easy to identify which is which, though there's frequently cross-over. Most of the weekend guests taking advantage of mini-vacation rates are leisure customers while the mid-week guests paying higher prices are business travelers. The hotel that wants to market to these customers in the future collects their names and addresses from their registration information and sends them news periodically about products and services they might enjoy.

Every business should develop a customer database by recording all the names and addresses of known customers — preferably in a computer where the information is organized in formatted files, and can be output as mailing labels. Ideally and eventually you'll want groups of e-mail addresses, organized according to interest.

A catalog mailing list is the beginning of a customer database. When customers are not yet identified, you can start building a mailing list by offering some kind of return incentive to the people who come in off the street. The reason local restaurants award free lunches to the winner of their weekly drawings is to collect those business cards or entry forms that tell them who their customers are. It's the same reason stores run "buy six, get one free" promotions, stamping a card for each purchase or recording your preferences in the computer register. The card usually has the customer's name and address; but the computer inventory system can go one better by recording what kind of coffee a customer buys most frequently or what kind of books s/he reads. Each example shows a company trying to get a better grip on who their customers are and what products and services they prefer.

In these days of 33-cent postage, and oceans of junk — excuse me — direct mail, you don't want to have to send more catalogs or postcards or newsletters than you have to. You want to send the right news to the right person.

A hotel doesn't want to send a brochure about their new meeting room to the retirees who stayed last summer while visiting their granddaughter. A performance speed shop doesn't want to send news about a new coil-over spring kit to a stock car racer whose class rules limit him to stock parts. That shop *would* want to know that customers have BMW 320i's if they've developed a new suspension component especially for that body-type. See why it's so important to know who will buy each product or service you offer?

It's one of the basic responsibilities of anyone selling something to someone else. Selling is not about cold calls and convincing people to pay for something they don't need. Selling is about identifying customer needs and presenting the information about your product or service in a way that makes sense to the customer. When the sales presentation is finished, the customer should know what that item will do for him or her, whether s/he buys it now, or later — or can't afford it at all!

It's critical to sell from the perspective of understanding what the prospective customer wants out of the deal. A codicil to this rule is "never assume." You might conclude that the sponsor of an event might want increased revenues from sales when actually what the company wants is visibility in its market area, brand recognition, positive associations with the event — all in the name of community relations rather than hard sales. The same is true of prospecting for PR clients. They may value positioning or awareness over how many items they can sell (see the section on evaluating sponsorship for more on this.) You must know what the sponsor's marketing needs are to answer them with your proposal.

Now you might say we've drifted off the course, here, talking about selling when we started out on the subject of identifying customers and developing mailing lists or databases. But we're not really putting the cart before the horse by talking about sales. Your best prospects are the customers who have already bought from you. Every company could increase sales by five percent by simply doing a better job of servicing the customers it already has. Since it costs much more to have to constantly go out and find new customers — especially if you are having to advertise all over the place to get them — doesn't it make sense to know who's already in hand?

Once the existing customer is profiled, there's the additional benefit of knowing another good customer when you see one. The more carefully you define the profile of your best customers, the more you have to go on when you look for others just like them.

So back to the database. Collect as much data as reasonably possible: name and address, past purchases, and anything about the systems or product those purchases were for. Additional information, such as:

- Are customers primarily interested in professional or hobby applications? Business or leisure?
- Are they high-end or budget?
- Is the customer a regular, or a one-time-only walk-in?
- What's the sales potential of each?
- Who are the customers to be targeted for more sales and who are the ones you wish would go away?
- Wholesalers need to ask, "Are the customers dealers for a particular interest group?" (IBM vs. Mac, MCI vs. ATT, Pepsi vs. Coke?)

Record every personalizing bit of information in the customer database files. Once organized, think about what it says, and what other information would be useful:

- Are there people who seem to come in only occasionally, but are knowledgeable, and potentially good customers?
- Where else do they shop; how can you compete more effectively?
- Are there customers who seem to be very connected with a local club or professional organization? Would giving them an incentive bring in some of their associates?
- Are there new products customers might want, but there's no way to tell?

Develop a brief questionnaire, and ask! When you're developing your Website, make sure you have a place to capture customer information and e-mail addresses.

Once all of the customer data is assembled, it will suggest that your business has several different types of customers. Group those customer types, decide where the gaps in the information are, and what other data you want. Then put together a postcard questionnaire that fills in the gaps, adds new information, and provides an offer good enough to get the customer to respond. Measure the results and update your database files.

For example: Your business is a bed and breakfast. You know the names and addresses of past customers, but not what brought them to the area or to your establishment. You would like to know what other B&Bs they've stayed in and what ones they enjoyed. If you're thinking about offering either tea or an honor bar in the afternoon, but you don't know what would be more popular, ask!

## Figure 3.1: Example of an Information-Gathering Questionnaire

Name: _____

Address (street and e-mail): _____

_____

Birthday: _____ Time of year you travel most often:_____

What types of lodging do you prefer for vacation?
(Please rank from 1, first choice to last)

    ___ Bed & breakfast     ___ Private home

    ___ Inn     ___ Independent hotel

    ___ Chain hotel     ___ Hostel

Where have you stayed in this area (please check all that apply):

___ Your B&B

___ List Competitors individually.

_____

_____

Do you belong to any of the following car or travel clubs ?

    ___ AAA     ___ ALA

    ___ Entertainment     ___ AARP

    ___ Priority One     ___ Other: _____

Please list all of our amenities you currently use or would like to: (List of services and facilities and those you're considering.)

_____

_____

_____

Bring this card to [NAME AND ADDRESS OF YOUR B&B] for a 10% discount on your next stay and the chance to win a free weekend (or similar offer).

Print out the postcards. You could create your master and then copy it onto postcard-size labels that you affix to postage-paid postcards available at the post office. You can also purchase four-up sheets of postcards with decorative borders from the stock letterhead catalogs or office supply stores.

You need to ask a variety of questions to get the information you need. Figure 3.1 is an example of a questionnaire. This questionnaire could also be used in the e-mail response page of your Website.

People hate junk mail and they are suspicious of mailing lists. Whenever you ask for information, you should pay for it by giving the customer something in return. The only way to keep a postcard like this from being "filed" with the rest of the junk mail is to give its recipient something s/he wants.

You won't get a 100 percent response, but the rule of thumb is that a cold-call mailing of any survey nets about a three percent response. A mailing to a known group can produce a 25 to 30 percent response. Be sure to keep some blank cards on the counter or desk for new customers to fill out to keep them in touch with new products and services offered in the future.

For a club, the database should include anyone who is interested in the cause or activity — fans (including your relatives), sponsors, potential sponsors, reporters who cover the event. Keep a supply of postcards in the glove compartment to add new names to the fan club. Sponsors will be very interested in this captive audience of people who are predisposed to listen — and to support the sponsors.

## *Permission Marketing*

Once you understand the concept of databases, you should move to the next step, an area that has come to be called *permission marketing*.

The idea is, rather than constantly bugging those you have identified as customers — whether they're still interested or not — you develop a dialogue with them by asking their permission. This is especially effective when you're dealing with Internet and e-mail customers because e-mail gives you every advantage of direct mail, without the price of postage. The more often you want to talk to these customers, the more focused you want to get with your message, the more perfect a solution e-mail becomes.

The concept used to be characterized as *relationship marketing* but now, with e-mail capabilities allowing ever greater personalization and customization of your communications, the philosophy is permission marketing: literally asking your audiences' permission to communicate with them.

Smart relationship marketers always built their initiatives on an exchange of commerce. If you give me your name and address (and business), I'll give you benefits: one free stay for every 10, one free lunch for every 20, and the like. Permission marketing carries the idea one step further. If you give me more information, or follow along with my marketing curriculum, I'll increase the rewards.

The Internet is an entirely new, and revolutionizing marketing medium — but only if you play by the rules of permission marketing. It's a totally logical extrapolation of the customer database logic. When consumers are bombarded by 3,000 messages per day, to say nothing of the interruptions in their work and private lives, a marketer who seeks to make an impression by interrupting further is operating with little in his favor. Alternatively, if a customer is willing to volunteer receptivity to your message, or pay a premium or subscription in exchange for peace and quiet (pay-per-view is an example) you have succeeded in getting him or her to pay attention to what you're saying. You have cut through the clutter.

But that's only the overture. The curtain isn't up, yet. For now that you have his or her attention, you had better have a good show. You need a marketing curriculum.

The best Websites are designed as such a curriculum. Just as with newsletters, there's always something new for the audience to see. The key to permission marketing with e-mail newsletters and other on-line marketing communications is to engage the individual with *sustainable commerce*. It's the same as sustainable development — a buzzword among those who want desperately to attract tourists to their neck of the rainforest, without destroying the natural resources the tourists have come to see. Sustainable commerce positions the relationship as the fragile environment it is: the deal is to market with the customer's best interest — instead of the company's, or at least in conjunction with the company's — at heart. Permission marketing is a process, not a conclusion. It is a sustainable relationship built on the exchange of a willing ear (eye, more often) for entertainment, enlightenment, and the cultivation of sufficient good feelings and trust that your audience will buy from you.

This is a point not to be underestimated. In this age, the one thing people don't have is time — that means they don't have time to research the options they need to have in order to be informed consumers. Permission marketing allows you to earn their trust — while plugging into their hindbrains via the credit you derive from taking the time to ask permission and become a reliable source of information and entertainment. The long-term result is a customer who can make an informed decision to purchase your product or service, and one who will not experience buyer's remorse. It's a particularly effective tool for high-ticket sales.

The loyalty marketing program loop is roughly 15 years old. Only a hand-ful of companies have recognized the challenges of database marketing, including the need for the human touch.

Among them are the complaints one focus group on database marketing in particular identified. One man had placed a number of orders for fruit during a holiday season. The next year, the merchant helpfully supplied all the names and addresses to help with his ordering. Unfortunately, the man explained when he called the customer service line, all those orders were placed as thank-you's to the surgeons and other medical personnel who had assisted his ill mother the year before. He would not be placing the same orders again. After the third attempt to get them to stop supplying this helpful list, he gave up.

In the hotel business, the quandary has always been whether to automati-cally greet the guest with a favorite beverage, only to discover the miner-al water — or scotch — was a one-time aberration in preference, now per-manently encoded on a database for eternal, undesirable, replication. We sometimes try to be smarter than we are. Permission marketing goes the next step. It gives you the infrastructure to ask. (And we're not talking about a Cray computer for the infrastructure. Even index cards will do!)

Instead of assuming that everyone who has been your customer wants to be your customer again, permission marketing demands that you ask them first. In the example of the postcard questionnaire in Figure 3.1, you've advanced to permission marketing. You are *asking* the customer to complete your survey and you are offering an incentive (the free weekend drawing) in exchange. What you do with that permission is the next criti-cal juncture. Smart marketers *keep* asking, and keep moving closer to the sale. You ask if they're still interested in hearing what you have to say. You keep your curriculum interesting enough for them to say yes. Ultimately they graduate to a sale — assuming you have crafted your curriculum to build in that direction.

Build to easy sales. Reward your customers with a by-invitation-only event so that you get to meet them face-to-face. Award an entry-level ben-efit, that leads to a more protracted, long-term relationship. Free dessert or wine gets them to try dinner. Fifth-night-free at your resort earns you four nights' revenue. A free set-up analysis and scaling may net consultancy to the race team. It's not hard to figure out what you're willing to give away in order to earn the business. The challenge is answering the question, "to whom." Permission marketing addresses that challenge.

The analogy holds for media relations. As one high-tech maven puts it, though the point applies in any industry, with the proliferation of media you now have to talk to 300 people, individually and regularly. That's not possible. It is if you've asked their permission to talk to them via e-mail or fax. The only way you'll get that permission is to earn it by giving them something they want in exchange for listening to your pitch. That something is a solid story, concrete facts, valid trends, interesting interview subjects and your own high standards for honesty and reliability. E-mail is revolutionary because it lets the recipient of your marketing message raise his hand to say "tell me more." That should be all you need.

The best form of marketing communications is always the custom-tailored pitch. By creating and maintaining databases and by perfecting permission marketing skills, you earn trust and develop the sorts of dialogues with your customers (be they end-users or media), that produce results. Plus, once you start keeping track of contacts in an organized, formalized manner, you can trace trends, gaps, and opportunities.

## Databases and Permission Marketing Checklist

❑ Do you capture names, addresses, phone, fax, and e-mail data?

❑ Do your media databases include personal names, not just "Editor"?

❑ Do you note preferences for future contact?

❑ Do you ask for permission to continue to contact, or keep data forever?

❑ Do you ask or tell?

❑ Do you update data often?

❑ Do you reward customers for their loyalty?

❑ Does your mail or e-mail contact include a call to action?

❑ Do you have a curriculum for talking to customers — constantly updating information?

❑ Do you respect the confidentiality of the information you collect?

# Newsletters — Print and E-Mail

The previous chapter on Customer Databases concludes that the more you know about your customers and what they buy, the easier it is to sell them more — and to find others like them. Since PR marketing, like sales is about identifying customer needs and presenting information about your product or service in a way that shows the customer you can answer those needs, you must develop a database listing all of your or your client's known customers, what they've bought, and whether they're buying for business or personal use. Personal information like birthdays can prove useful, too. It's valuable to give something back to those on your list in exchange for the information they've provided via a business card drawing, or a discount coupon in exchange for filling out your questionnaire.

This chapter talks about another customer incentive which also serves the purpose of giving your customer more information about what you do and/or sell. That incentive and information piece is a core tool for marketing communications: the newsletter.

## What's In It for Your Reader?

Take the example of any newsletter you currently receive. Even better, pull out a recent copy and look at it critically as you consider the following purposes for a newsletter:

- Shows the current or potential customer some of the sender's inside thinking;
- Educates you about what's important in the industry or area of interest; and
- Advertises products and services.

Now that you've developed a database, you can use it at its most simple level to create mailing lists of your customers. Consider what you could do in a newsletter. You can:

- Share your inside thinking on whatever you do best.
- Educate your customer about what's happening in the marketplace.
- Promote what's new in your shop.
- Make your customers feel like they're part of your team.
- Keep media who follow your industry informed.

You'll notice that each of these items applies whether you sell professional consulting services, gourmet dining or craftware.

Getting back to the bit about offering customers an incentive, you do that by simply giving them free information. Everyone likes to be on the inside; and that's what your newsletter should do. On top of that, because you're distributing this newsletter just to known buyers, you could include some kind of coupon in the pages. A coupon is a call to action, which brings the customer back to your office or store. If you include a copy of your newsletter in every order to new customers, that coupon might turn a one-time customer into a repeat buyer. Add a free subscription form in your counter or mail order copies, and you'll be able to send the next issue to them, with another call to action and so on.

The airlines did it first — and best — when they started frequent flyer programs. The whole purpose of these things was to get passengers names and addresses — to build a database, cross-referencing where they flew so that the airline could tell them about new routes, fares and promotions. Most of them did it — and still do — with a newsletter.

When the frequent flyer programs started out, all the airlines had for passenger information was a name, not even an address, as most tickets went through a travel agency and carried their, or a company's address. The same was true for hotels. Marriott's Honored Guest program was designed to identify Marriott's customers and which hotels they used in order to provide them with information about new hotels, programs, and promotions they might use. It's pretty easy to figure out that neither hotels nor airlines got into the frequent traveler games to give away hotel rooms and airline tickets. So this database marketing must be pretty powerful stuff. And it is.

## *Inform, Educate, Promote*

Database marketing lets you give your customer what s/he needs though neither of you may know what that is at the start. By sending your newsletter, you showcase what's best about your business: projects you're working on, news about recent acquisitions or lines, tips on how to use your operation to its best advantage, the personalities behind the people on your front (and back) benches. By sending a newsletter, you offer information in a non-threatening manner, and gain the credibility that a news story offers over an ad. By sending a newsletter you stay in touch with your customers — in a highly cost-effective manner.

A word about the format and the costs. Everything that Chapter 2 described about brochures applies to newsletters. Keep it — language and design — simple and easy to read. Keep it short and entertaining. Make sure you include your name, address, phone, fax, and 800 number. Include your e-mail address, if you have one. In fact, you could offer your newsletter via e-mail if you have your customers' e-mail addresses.

Don't worry about color and typesetting — you can produce the newsletter copy on the same computer you keep your mailing list on, and either scan in photos or drawings, or do a simple cut-and-paste with your copy machine.

You can punch up your cut-and-paste photos by asking your local printer to make PMT prints of your glossy photos — they reproduce better. You can produce a perfectly wonderful newsletter by copying onto both sides of an 11" x 17" sheet of white paper, and folding it in half, book-style, and then again in thirds, letter-style. If you leave the lower third of your back page blank except for a return address, you'll now have a blank space for your mailing label and the postage will be the same as for a letter. Total production cost? As little as $.20 each (or as little as $1 per piece for basic four-color printing on one side).

If you keep it simple, you'll do it often. A newsletter should go out often enough to be newsy — ideally once a month, but at least once a quarter.

As you build your customer base and start identifying niche groups, you can start creating specialty inserts for the newsletter just for that crowd.

The shell will cover the same news for everyone, but the insert will tell about specialty products or services for them, offer a special promotion, or announce a special event you're sponsoring for that interest group. Again, the more specific you can make your sales pitch — the more you can identify your capabilities with your customer's needs — the more impact it will have, and the more sales you'll make.

## The Annual Report Newsletter

A year-end newsletter can also serve as an annual report. If you've taken a look at any corporate annual reports lately, you've seen some exciting graphics and great photography. Your annual report, newsletter, or magazine should capture the excitement of your business, too. You don't need to spend tons of money. Just use some color as an accent and make the design punchy. There are other applications for a year-end newsletter as well, such as a newsletter for small company investors who are interested in the success of a business but do not expect a formal report where none is required. An annual report newsletter is also a great way for an independent PR professional to report on the highlights of the year in a format which becomes an additional piece of sales collateral on future prospecting calls.

In terms of content, think about what you have accomplished, at the level of detail your reader (such as a future customer) can appreciate. What have you done this year to attract customers, increase awareness in the market, and help the company relate better to employees, customers or distributors? Using the example of a race team to point up how any business working on another's behalf could report the year's activities:

- Did you take the show car to a distributor's warehouse(s)? Make sure you list every stop in your report; then forward copies of the printed piece to all those distributors.

- Did you go up in the stands or to a hospitality tent to visit with attendees or sign autographs? What did that mean to the kids, or sponsor's guests who were there? Do you have a photograph or a quote you can include?

- How many miles did your team cover this season? Assuming your hauler has your sponsor(s) names on it, how much exposure, and in what geographic areas (markets) did; your traveling billboard receive?

- Naturally you want to include the highlights of your publicity — and of course there isn't room to include every clipping. One technique for showcasing the best of your PR is to create a broadside, which is a collage of headlines, photos, and extracts from great stories. If you treat this collection as an illustration in your newsletter, you'll get the point across that this is just a sampling of all the coverage. This technique also works well if there wasn't much publicity. Leave your readers with the impact of the most positive stories.

- If your series was televised, make sure you emphasize how many viewers the program had — and the equivalent in advertising exposure your team got, if you have that information available

- The purpose of this exercise is to document the value your sponsor(s) received for the dollars they invested in your team. In essence, every public relations report is doing the same thing — detailing the benefits the client received for the money spent on professional PR services.

- When you're tallying up the results, including the wins and the crowd who saw the car and your sponsor's logo at every race, figure out how many races you ran, how many fans were in attendance, and what demographics those tracks drew. Don't forget to include all the collateral bits you used: that driver's uniform and matching shoes in your sponsor's colors which took $1,000 or so out of the sponsorship funds, plus the cost of painting the car, and hauler, also the driver's cards and press kits you printed.

The average marketing committee doesn't know, unless you tell them, where the money went. They can't make an intelligent decision about that sponsorship, or whether to be your client next year unless they can measure the return on investment.

If you put together this report to your stakeholders, you can demonstrate why, even if you didn't win the championship or put your client on the front page of the *Wall Street Journal*, your overall marketing performance produced winning results.

## E-Mail Newsletters

While the Internet and e-mail are established marketing media, how many teams and businesses are taking advantage of the traditional and leading-edge opportunities these new communication vehicles allow? You may not even understand the distinction between e-mail and the

Internet — and the ways to leverage each one on behalf of your team, business, or sponsor. Consider the implications of the prediction that nearly half of the U.S. population, or roughly 135 million people, will communicate by e-mail by 2001.

The best thing about e-mail is that you're more likely to be able to reach your target audiences. So how do you reach them? By letting them know how to e-mail *you*.

The biggest difference between having a Website and offering e-mail communication through your Website is that e-mail is, by definition, interactive. Websites on the Internet should be interactive in some dimension (an "e-mail us with your questions" page, for example); but not all are. NASCAR.com, for many, is more important as an electronic source and outlet for news about motorsports, than as a chat room. Websites are basically infomercials that the surfer reviews when and where s/he chooses. Your own Website needs to be designed so it's entertaining, easy to navigate, fast, and informative. In that order. If you're a retail entity, why wouldn't you set up your Website as a Webstore?

E-mail, on the other hand, is a combination of the telephone and the letter. The immediacy is unbeatable. The format allows for a lengthier, more detailed message than you'd want to leave as voicemail, plus it prompts response in the form of a specific answer, instead of the frustration of telephone tag. With e-mail, you know what the mailer wants, and you can answer. With voice mail one of the great frustrations is people who call — or return calls — without telling you what they're calling for!

The relative novelty of e-mail can still work in your favor, although the sheer volume of e-mail people receive is quickly erasing this advantage. For the PR marketer this means that there's a slightly better chance an editor will respond to your e-mail while getting through on the phone may be impossible. As one editor put it, "If I don't respond to your e-mail, take a hint! Don't bombard me with calls, faxes, and more e-mails."

## E-Mail Distribution

The first way to build an address book of e-mail addresses is to include your e-mail address, as well as your Website if it has an interactive page, in all your communications. Make sure you get e-mail addresses when you ask customers and contacts for mailing addresses and phone numbers.

Many of the media directories include e-mail addresses for editors. But you'll find that the best way to establish e-mail communications with editors is to ask. Apply the fax rule — don't do it unless you have received the okay.

Collect e-mail addresses through your Website — an ideal approach is to offer answers to questions in your area of specialization. If you have this capability but you're not getting any traffic, try www.did-it.com, which will survey the search engines — for free — to find out whether your Website is listed. Do not assume that because someone set up a site for you that they listed it with the search engines. Registering the name is not the same thing. Once you establish yourself in the search engines, you can promote your Website through a variety of means, including the Internet News Bureau (www.newsbureau.com/digest), which for a minimal fee will announce your site to roughly 2,000 publications who cover new sites. Your Website is a service to your customers and prospective customers. You have to promote it the same way you would any other service — or no one will know you're there.

Back to e-mail and the doors you can open with it. Each Monday morning when I check my e-mail I will have four e-mail newsletters waiting for me:

- *Travel Management Daily*: which supplies news and trends on the travel industry.
- *Web-Promote*: a free weekly briefing on, as you'd imagine, marketing on the Internet. (Their e-mail: newsletter@webpromote.com)
- *EventWeb*: a free weekly newsletter on using e-mail and Websites to promote attendance at meetings and conferences. (Their e-mail: dougfox@eventweb.com)
- *MADSearch*: a free weekly newsletter advising meeting planners of available group hotel space (for hotel clients who have the facilities meeting planners need). (Their e-mail: MADSearch1@aol.com)

You can create an e-mail newsletter for just about any business: a restaurant, a team or a hotel, using the "News" page on their Website repackaged in an e-mail format to send to clients.

## Advantages to E-Mail Newsletters

There are several advantages to using e-mail to distribute your newsletter:

- Immediacy: There's no lead time for printing. You can write it and get it to your readers on the same day. You can update the news as frequently as you want; the rule of thumb seems to be weekly.

- Simplicity: All you have to work with is basic type. You can't even underline or italicize and there's no capability for graphics. The best you can do is a ":)" or an 800-FLOWERS "-<-<-@."
- Cost: Virtually none: no printing, color, postage, or data-processing.
- Impact: Because the recipient has asked you to send your e-mail newsletter, s/he is much more likely to read, or at least skim it. S/he has given you permission to send your newsletter — something we don't always have when it comes to printed newsletters — and is therefore much more receptive to the information. It is likely that because the recipient is focused, s/he's settled at the PC, at the office or at home, prepared to read the e-mail, and there are no graphics distractions, the content actually registers. If you're smart, you'll break up the text with sub-heads so it is easy to read, and you should follow the syntax of e-mail by keeping the sentences almost telegram-short. E-mail encourages people to follow that old time-management advice: touch each piece of paper that crosses your desk only once. People would rather read and then delete the e-mail message than come back to it.

Permission marketing starts with e-mail newsletters, e-mail messages, and press releases to editors. The new technology allows us to get buy-in for whatever we're trying to accomplish by easily asking, may I? The acknowledgment of your prospect's privacy alone goes straight to that hind-brain and makes your audience more willing to believe what you have to say.

Whether you take the traditional printed route, which has the advantage of permanence and the psychographic benefits that comes from using pictures, design, and color, or if you choose the interactivity and immediacy of e-mail newsletters, both are an important basic tool in your PR marketing arsenal.

CHAPTER

5

# Press Releases and Press Kits

The press release is the basic tool for compiling the information on any given subject you want to communicate to the media. It's the vehicle that gathers up all the performance components and carries your news to the finish line. The more professionally you put it together, the more likely it will get to the finish line first and win the race for publicity.

## Appearance

Believe it or not, editors say that it's important for your press release to look good. In the editor's eyes, this means that not only should the grammar and spelling be perfect, not only should it be readable (no fuzzy copies, dot matrix printing, or tiny close-together type), it should be on appealing stationery, too. While this may seem to be totally frivolous, there are three good reasons why this is not just preference but necessity:

1. A nicely packaged press release adds credibility to your message. If you don't care enough about the way your news looks, maybe you don't care about its accuracy, either.

2. A colorful logo, or interesting-looking envelope will stand out in the crowd, since what you must accomplish first is getting the editor to open your letter.

3. Editors and reporters will start recognizing your releases, they'll stand out in the piles of paper they receive each day.

You can invest a few hundred dollars in letterhead and have it serve both your business letter needs and as press release paper. Whatever color or graphics you choose, make sure you can still easily read the letter or news. In this era of faxes, it's also important that the background color doesn't turn the page black or that your logo doesn't disappear when you fax it. Embossed logos used to be the sign of ritzy companies. No longer — the embossed symbol doesn't show up when you fax it.

Once you have the paper your press release will be printed on, make sure you have access to a typewriter or word processor so your information is neat and easy-to-read. How you place your news on the page is just as important. The following tips apply:

- Make the type as easy to read as possible. The typeface in books and most magazines is what we all learned to read on. Use a serif type-face, it's the one with the little tails on all the letters. To the American eye, serif type and upper- and lower-case letters, is easier to read. Don't write your press release in all-capital letters.

- Double-space the lines. Again, this makes your news easier to read.

- Try to keep your information to one page, or two, max. Editors don't have time to wade through long press releases.

- If you do go to two pages, write "—more—" at the bottom of page one and "key word-2" at the top of the second page, in case the two pages get separated. The key word can either be your name or the topic of the news.

- At the end of your press release, write "30" or "###." This convention in the news biz tells the reader that it's the end of the release.

- On every release, in addition to your company name, address, phone, fax, and e-mail numbers that are printed on your letterhead, you should always note a contact name and phone number where that person can be reached.

- It also helps to note whether your news is, "For Immediate Release" or "For use before XXX deadline." For example, if you are announcing an open house, the news will be old if it's not used before the date of your event, put a "use by" date at the top. Make sure you're getting your releases in the mail in time to meet the editors' deadlines.

# Razzle-Dazzle!

How do you get the editor to notice your envelope in the stacks of mail on his or her desk? Ever notice how the extra-shiny race car, or the extra-snazzy graphics get even more attention, even when the other cars and drivers are pretty evenly matched? You have to make your press release stand out. In an environment like this, it can take sending someone a cake to get them to even read your press release (even open the envelope!) about a new restaurant menu. It can mean, with the *New York Times*, for example, "don't call us, we'll call you."

Even if the editor you work with always uses your releases, it never hurts to have fun with the process. Razzle-dazzle a little. Send him or her a three-dimensional symbol of whatever your news is. Send red, plush, fuzzy lobsters to the editors you're sending a lobster bake press release and get instant recognition from every person you call to find out if they're coming to the press preview. When was the last time you threw away a package or a padded envelope, unopened?

# Content

You've got a nice looking car on the track. The paint is clean and shiny. The sponsors' names are spelled correctly. It meets all the rules of the class for size and weight. But the nicest car in the world won't get you to the finish line without some muscle under the hood, the right aerodynamics, and a carefully planned race strategy. Your news release needs news.

## What's News?

What's news? Selling your news to an editor is just like selling any other product — you have to tell your customers what's in it for them. In the news business, you have to sell the editor information: news that readers can use that makes them take interest and respond by continuing to pay attention to the newspaper, magazine column, or TV show. Every time you think about sending out a press release, you must answer the question, "Who cares?"

The news can be completely esoteric, as long as you're sharing it with other people who are interested in what you have to say. Package your news for the appropriate audience you want to reach, and then identify the reporters and editors who cover that niche.

The news content is the engine. The stronger the news, backed up by facts, the further your release will go. The appropriateness of your news for the editor you've mailed it to is the angle you take — how you explain why the news is important. When you're explaining why your news is important, you need to back it up with hard facts or, if they're opinions rather than facts, they need to be attributed to someone so the reader can decide whether s/he believes that person or not. It's an unfortunate reality that if you baldly state, "Business X is the leader in this field," you're inviting disbelief. But if you say, "According to customer Y, 'Business X exceeded my expectations for product, service, and quality by sending me the parts I needed overnight,'" or even, "Business owner X commented, 'We really believe we offer a unique service to our customers,'" you're substantiating your information.

As PR person you are the information officer for your company. You have to explain what you are doing in order to position your client as the one who's doing it best, providing all the facts and background information that put your story in context.

## Turning Features into Benefits

There's quite a bit involved in "providing all the information that puts your story in context." Consider this example. A reporter calls and asks, "What's new in The Islands of The Bahamas? Is there hotel news that meeting planners will be interested to know?" You might answer with three pages of detail about the new hotels being built. But that would answer only part of the question. The reporter had asked "what's new that *meeting planners* should know about." While the construction is new, the first answer didn't explain why the new construction and renovations would interest meeting planners. It failed to translate the features into benefits.

This is Rule Number One in selling, and PR marketing is selling in the truest sense. You must translate features into benefits. The best salespeople, therefore the best PR marketing practitioners, are active negotiators not passive order-takers. They seek to understand their customers and ask what their needs are before presenting answers and products. This holds true whether you're asking a client for the business order, a reporter for coverage, or a company for sponsorship

What do you have to offer that the customer wants? How can you make your solution, answers, or products fit his or her needs? The best way to

**Figure 5.1: Discerning Between Features and Benefits**

| Using the meeting planner inquiry as the example, try to define which is a Feature and which is a Benefit: | Feature | Benefit |
| --- | --- | --- |
| 1. The hotel is adding 300 rooms | ❏ | ❏ |
| 2. The hotel can now accommodate groups of up to 500 | ❏ | ❏ |

explain the difference between features and benefits is to offer a short quiz as in Figure 5.1.

In this pair, the first is a feature — what do those rooms mean to meeting planners? Bigger groups? More professionalism from the staff? A better rooms product for guests?

The second example answers the question: how does this work to my advantage? It's a benefit statement.

Try the exercise again in Figure 5.2.

**Figure 5.2: Discerning Between Features and Benefits**

| Using the meeting planner inquiry as the example, try to define which is a Feature and which is a Benefit: | Feature | Benefit |
| --- | --- | --- |
| 1. Our calipers are 10 lbs. lighter than our competitor's. | ❏ | ❏ |
| 2. We supply two sets of brake pads. | ❏ | ❏ |
| 3. Research shows that NASCAR fans are 72% more likely to support sponsors — two to three times more so than other sports fans | ❏ | ❏ |
| 4. "Coca Cola refreshes NASCAR." | ❏ | ❏ |
| 5. "Drink accordingly." | ❏ | ❏ |

Both of these are product features. The first statement starts moving toward a benefit because the customer could interpret that significantly lighter calipers are better for performance cars. The second statement doesn't explain why there are two sets. Do they wear out faster? Are there two different types of pads, allowing (as is the case here) the team to fine-tune the brake bias just by changing pads. You must understand your customer's knowledge and comprehension. Translating features into benefits doesn't have to be at Kindergarten level, it just has to make the connection back to what's in it for the buyer. Don't underestimate a consumer's suspicions. They have come to be very cynical about advertising doublespeak. "New and improved" usually means "not as good as the old stuff." If you don't define the positive, the customer will jump to a negative conclusion — like your calipers somehow wear out brake pads.

The third statement is a clear-cut benefit and it's definitive. Wherever you can cite hard research and independently confirmed statistics to support your benefit statement you enhance credibility. Remember, when you're writing press releases, that unsupported opinion does not qualify as news. If you have to say the team is great, at least put the words in the mouth of your owner, crew chief, or driver. Preferably, have him or her say something more specific. "Great" is a feature; "we expect to be competitive because we've been practicing the pit stops we messed up last week" gives fans and jaded motorsports writers the benefit of tagging along to see if you're right.

Statements 4 and 5 are a very interesting sequence in advertising Coca Cola's sponsorship of the 50th NASCAR anniversary. Statement 4 translates the feature that Coca Cola is a beverage into the benefit that it is a "refreshing" beverage, then trumps its own benefit statement with the play on words, "refreshes NASCAR" designed to tell those 72 percent loyal NASCAR fans that Coca Cola is on their team. The punch-line, "Drink accordingly" makes sure the consumer gets that benefit point and even asks for the sale.

## Psychological Ramifications of Benefit Statements

The benefit statement provides context by supplying enough details for the recipient to draw conclusions — which is what you want: an active participant in your sales equation. The HBO program *From the Earth to the Moon*, provided a great example of the importance of context. Professor Lee Silver from Cal Tech was trying to teach the Apollo 15, 16, and 17 crews who would be exploring the lunar surface how to look for the right rocks — the ones that would be useful, scientifically, to draw conclusions about the origins of lunar geology. The context in which the rocks were found — the terrain, geological history deduced from their surroundings and similarity (or dissimilarity) to surrounding rocks — all contributed to drawing a richer profile of the sample. As Professor Silver supposedly said, "Give me a dead cat and all I can tell you is that it's a cat and it's dead. Tell me you found the cat in the middle of the road, and my conclusions will head in one direction. Tell me you found it in the middle of the kitchen of your favorite restaurant and I'll go in a different direction."

Benefit statements are context. They allow your customer to draw conclusions and form opinions, which is exactly what you want. Put the information in the proper context, with factual benefit statements and your customers will follow the trail you've laid out and discover the conclusion you lead them to. Without context, the features just lie there, like rocks on a lab table.

The other interesting thing about translating features into benefits is that it has very complex psychological ramifications. When customers have engaged in the exchange, they'll be more likely to believe the conclusion they've drawn because they took an active role in its development.

In PR, by providing the requested information in a format the reporter can immediately use, the same psychological advantage applies — plus you've made it easy for him or her by doing the leg-work. Build relationships with reporters via frequent contact and dialogue. Engage them appropriately often in the sales pitch process and supply the information product they need. Identify yourself to them as the source of trend and background information — context. The bonus is that when you supply the context — a choice over which you can have full control — you can easily and honestly direct the story back to your team, product, or service.

## *Publicity Strategy*

The most basic strategy is, "we want to get as much publicity as we can." So you send out a press release and get yourself in front of the trade photographer every chance you get. The problem with this approach is that you can wear out your welcome. You can run out of steam. You can crash by doing something really stupid like reporting news that isn't quite true. Or you can be one of those in the back of the pack who's always out there, but never seems to deliver. The better approach is to pace yourself. Establish an early identity, then watch for opportunities to develop where you can show your stuff. Make the envelope with your press release the sign of a guaranteed performer, full of real, informative news, every time out of the chute. By earning respect and credibility from your media contacts, you gain a professional edge.

There's also the more important tactical question. Some people believe the traditional press release is all but dead as a printed-hard-copy-mailed-to-an-editor. However, the electronic press release sent by e-mail is thriving. The reason? You've done the legwork. If the editor's interested in your story, all s/he has to do is highlight and clip your copy and paste it into the publication on-line.

Anyone who writes knows that short-cuts are appreciated — it's easier to do a cut-and-paste on the computer than to re-type or re-write perfectly good copy. It's also a perfectly acceptable efficiency, when you're writing pitch letters focused on the same needs-benefits message, to ensure personalization on each letter while copying the core information. Good e-mail press releases deliver benefits to your editor-customer on two levels: they supply useful information in applicable context, and do so in a format that is efficient for the editor to use.

## Publicist as Information Officer

Always keep in mind just how few people there are out there who understand your specialty — whatever it is — and how much education needs to be done if you are to further your professional success and the opportunities for your clients.

As professionals, we have a responsibility to educate not just our current fans and customers — the people who are already interested in what we do and need to be kept loyal — but also to tell our story in a professional manner to those who could be our fans and customers. Remember those in a variety of media who speak to those fans and customers. It's part of the job.

In every industry, the role of the PR person is really information officer. You have to explain what you, your team, or your company is doing in order to position your client as the one who's doing it best. And you can't complain about how someone covers your client unless you provide all the facts and background information that put your story in context.

# *Press Kits*

Press kits still make sense in this Internet era to provide background information in a format that is efficient for the editor and for you, the PR person. Editors will rarely wade through a fat press kit. That is why I don't believe in mailing press kits except when all the information in them is new, or when you're dealing with a press corps that has never heard of you. By assembling the facts at your disposal in separate contexts, one for each audience of customers, you'll have something set to fax or e-mail out when a reporter calls you, on deadline, on a Friday afternoon.

Think of a press kit as a reporter's desk reference on your operation. If s/he has a question about what you do, or a detail of your product, the press kit should: 1) have the answer; and 2) be somewhere that's easy to find.

Some press kits include company brochures, copies of articles, and pages from other sources detailing the company's history. You'd think these press kits fit the definition because, like the spaghetti sauce "it's in there" — any detail or fact you want to know is there, somewhere. But often these kits fail the second criterion — they don't make it quick and easy for reporters to find what they're looking for. They're like a tool box full of a jumble of things — and the reporter, who's always in a hurry because the deadline looms, doesn't have time to look through everything in the box. S/he needs the right tool, fast, and wants to simply go to the drawer marked "wrenches" and pick out the right size.

## What the Press Kit Should Contain

To hold the information, all you need is a nice looking, sturdy two-pocket folder. Put a logo or sticker on it for identification, and affix a business card inside. Press kit covers can include four-color printing, special die-cuts and folds for tabs so that it can be used as a file folder. There are even business cards designed as Rolodex cards that pop up when you open the folder. But all that window-dressing is more flash, and more expensive, than you really need. Use your resources appropriately to make sure the press kit serves you in appearance and functionality. Don't let form get in the way of function.

### Fact Sheet

First, and on the top of the pile of papers in the right hand pocket of the press kit folder there should be a fact sheet. The fact sheet should contain the company name and address and the contact person's name, phone number, e-mail, and fax. The fact sheet should also include key personnel, such as the president/CEO, financial officer, vp's, director of marketing, or owner. This listing is primarily to give the reporter a reference for checking the spelling of someone's name.

The fact sheet should contain key facts and figures — number of locations or products, number of employees, gross annual sales or other business-size reference, and a one-sentence descriptor that the reporter can use. An example is: "Based in New Hampshire, Leading Edge Motorsport serves the owners and drivers of performance cars, focusing on braking systems, suspension/steering and the car-driver interface." This sentence should sum up who you are (or what you do) and what distinguishes you, either in the industry, or from your competitors. A geographic locator such as "based in," or "headquartered in," gives readers a reference point when they come looking for you. The fact sheet is the single most important element in the press kit. Everything else you put in there should supply supporting detail to those facts.

## Backgrounder or Company History

The "backgrounder" or company history is ideally presented in a quick-scan format for the reporter looking for the date the company was founded or the date a particular product or process was introduced. The chronology style of company history also shows growth, highlights milestones, and keeps you from risking the preparation of either a too-dull or too-chatty narrative history. The purpose of a backgrounder in a press kit is to provide quick facts that will be inserted in another story. It is not a stand-alone record of everything your company has done and credit for every minute detail. If you're taking the backgrounder or company history from the corporate brochure or yearbook, at least highlight the important parts — or prepare a one-page extract.

## Supporting Data

A press kit should also contain:

- A press release explaining your industry and your niche in it, with a brief description of what you do and why you're the expert.
- Individual press releases for each type of customer (market segment) you seek; detailing the products and services you offer each niche and why you do it better than your competition.
- A release that explains your product or services' features and benefits in engineering or technical terms.
- A constantly-updated news release about recent developments in your company, special events, new products, or services. This release

should contain a brief paragraph about who you are, how you can be reached, and what niche you occupy.

A publicity kit for a personality would focus on the last two categories, with a fresh news release each week of performance season. The head sheet models and actors use to detail their credentials might suffice for a fact sheet. Your press kit would also contain:

- The personality's biography;
- Brief introduction copy for anyone who needs to introduce him or her;
- A release about a fan club, Website, and other special team programs (for example, charity involvement, newsletters, and souvenirs); and
- Releases detailing human interest stories about the personality to help psychologically position the people on the crew as positive ambassadors.

The press releases should act like chapters in a book. Each chapter covers a different subject — and each should have a title that describes it. For example, if a trade reporter is looking for a description of your specialization for that industry, s/he can find it in the release with the headline, "XYZ Consulting Offers Tax Tools for Graphic Artists." Each product your company manufactures, or each line your store sells should have its own release that presents the features and benefits, applications, and price or price range. The press kit for Omni Hotels contained a release on weekend packages, a release on meeting and group capabilities, one on Select Guest, the frequent traveler program, one on ESP, the corporate travel program, one of the development plans for the company, and one on the historic hotels in the collection. You need to answer the reporter's basic questions with press kit information.

- What is it?
- How does it work?
- Why is it different?
- Where can I get it?
- How much does it cost?

These are the questions the reader has, so they are the answers (who, what, where, when, why) the reporter needs to find in your press kit. Your press releases should be accompanied by technical charts or graphs and black and white product and people photos. As you can see, if you have these releases in easy reach, and you can figure out what your press customer is likely to be asking for, you'll save yourself a scramble. The discipline also allows you to stay on the leading edge of the curve, and causes you to find stories that you might not have recognized.

Finally, there's the area of clips from other sources. You include copies of good publicity for one main reason: to add credibility to your pitch. Obviously, if the *New York Times* thinks you're newsworthy, every other publication you approach will think so too. But it's also true for the trade magazines, that if one publication writes about you, the others will, too.

Be very careful about clips. Never alter the story by cutting and pasting your way up the column. Include the entire story — with your mention highlighted if you need to focus the reader's attention — and don't cut off headlines. If the object is to demonstrate that another publication thinks you're news, then you'll want to make sure the name and date of the magazine or newspaper article appears on the clip.

Many trade publications are happy to reprint your article at minimal cost. They'll even take out the ads and insert your own address or contact information so you can use the piece in your direct mail program. Reprints cover all the issues: copyrights, date, identification, and making sure the article appears in its original format.

Make sure to keep your press kit as current as you can. Check the dates on your press releases and clips to make sure there's something current in there and it's not a folder full of year-old news.

## When To Send a Press Kit and When Not To

A word about distribution:

- You should not mail out press kits every time you send out a release.
- You should send out press kits if you have never done one and want to make sure all your media contacts have the facts they need. Hand them out at trade shows to the people who cover your industry; or send them with a cover letter, that includes the latest piece of news on your operation and a comment like, "I'm enclosing a current press kit so you can update your file on us."
- Have a supply on hand any time you hold a special event like an open house so you can hand them to any media who attend.

The idea is that press kits go to reporters who seem pretty likely to write about you. The press kit lets them check their facts. When you send out a press release, it's not certain that any article will come out of all the places you've distributed it. The editor of a new product roundup doesn't need a press kit to edit the press release you've sent. Editors and reporters are already drowning in the mail they receive. Don't make it worse by sending the great American novel to someone who needs just a sound bite. Save the paper, postage, and aggravation by reserving press kits for those who really want them.

The press kit is the portable — and accessible — encyclopedia on who you are. Make sure it tells your story, and provide it only when it will actually be used (as well as anytime anyone asks you for one). Make yours a kit for building a good, solid story and it will become a tool that makes your job easier.

## Tracking Publicity Results

The purpose of a press release is mainly to provide your contact with information to be used in a future column or as the basis for a future story. Your effectiveness as a PR person is judged by those results, so it makes sense to talk a bit about how you anticipate, track, and measure media pick-up. In the case of feature stories, most are prepared with your full knowledge. A story requires follow-up from the writer, to set up interviews, secure photographs, and other types of contact that let you know a story is in the works. When that happens, you know to be on the lookout for the publication, and it's certainly okay to ask the reporter when the story might appear.

Press release-based stories are much more elusive prey. Generally, if you're part of a particular industry, you're reading most of the trade publications. If you've sent a release to the trades you'll know when and where to look for it. When you're working for a consumer client, like a hotel, restaurant, or other general news product, you have much more ground to cover. Few people have access to every daily newspaper on the distribution list. That's where clipping services come in. For a couple of hundred dollars a month, their people read newspapers and magazines, and clip every story that your client's name appears in. In addition to the monthly fee, they charge you per clip and send you the actual clipping with a little label noting the name of the publication and its circulation.

Luce and Burrelle's are the national services. Video and radio monitoring services are also available. These services cover virtually every publication likely to carry your story, including your industry's trades, and will clip for whatever key words and names you want. It is smart to be careful when choosing your key words unless you want to pay a dollar per clip every time your hotel is listed in a business journal calendar because it's the main meeting venue in town. Of course if you want to spend lots of money, you could have your clipping service read for your competitor's name, too, and then compare your results to theirs.

The more meaningful way to use a clipping service is to analyze the impact of the stories about your company or client. You can either pay the service for what's called a clip analysis, or you can do it yourself. A clip analysis quantifies the pick-up you receive according to several scales. You can choose as many as you want, but the basic ones are:

- How many clips, with what circulation and what value?
- How much impact did the mention have?
- What type of publication is giving the most attention?

The first category is straightforward. As noted, the clipping service tells you the circulation for each publication clipped. To get the number of clips and total circulation, just tally up the clippings. Frequently, this is part of the clipping service. To find out the monetary value of the publicity, you need to know what the ad rate per column inch is for each publication. Then you multiply the rate by the length of your clip and have an equivalent advertising value for your story. It's up to you whether you add a premium to that value to reflect the greater impact of editorial over advertising placements. Some of the major PR agencies put a three-times factor to the value of their clips.

## Rating PR Placement

To measure psychological impact a different way, you can rate the type of placement in advance, and categorize the clips. This allows you to say, for example, that even a short (three-inch) feature story with your company name in the headline has more impact than a three-inch mention in a more general roundup. You can subdivide the categories further by rating consumer stories higher than trade stories. The rule of thumb for a hotel company, therefore, might be:

5-points: Feature story, consumer
4-points: Roundup, consumer

3-points: Feature story, trade

2-points: Roundup story, trade

1-point: Mention

In addition to reporting your clips by awarding them the corresponding point values, you could prepare a pie chart showing the proportion of the clips of each value to each other.

To measure the types of publications carrying your news, you can prepare another pie chart that compares, for example, the number of trade stories to the number of consumer stories, or the number of trade roundup stories to the trade features. This chart shows you — and your client — at a glance whether you're getting the balance of coverage you seek.

Thick stacks of clippings are nice. Framed displays or broadsides of the stories with the best headlines or photos are gratifying on your office or shop wall — and are subtle reminders to visitors that you're doing something that at least some reporters find fascinating. But the professional publicist wants more detail. By analyzing your clips, you can tell where your efforts are succeeding. You can tell which publications are using the information you provide and which aren't. Then you can do something concrete to improve the areas that are lacking. If you have only the vague sense that one of the publications that reports on your industry hasn't done a story on your company, and you complain to the editor, only to find out they did one three months ago, the one time you didn't see the magazine, you'll feel like an idiot. But if you take the proactive approach and mention the lack of coverage to an editor while you're relating a great bit of news, the chances are good that the editor will be surprised they haven't and flattered that you pay so much attention to the publication.

Aside from these benefits, being able to quantify your results to whomever pays you for your efforts, even linking your compensation to the results you produce, will set you apart as a professional. That type of making a splash is always rewarding!

## *Press Release Checklist*

1. Make it look good

   ❑ Letter head for professional appearance and editor recognition.

   ❑ Colorful logo or interesting-looking envelope.

❑ Typed addresses, not labels.

2. Format and style

❑ Easy-to-read typeface.

❑ Upper- and lower-case, not all upper-case.

❑ Double-spaced.

❑ Keep it to two pages.

❑ Write "—more—" at the bottom of the first page and "keyword - 2" on the next.

❑ At the end of the release, write, "###."

❑ Include a contact name, phone number, and e-mail.

❑ Note whether news is "For Immediate Release" or "Release on xx/xx/xx."

3. What's news?

❑ Address the information to the audience who will care about it.

❑ Identify editors and reporters who cover your niche.

❑ Back up the news with facts, trends, and context.

❑ Attribute opinions to persons you quote. Don't editorialize.

4. Strategy

❑ Pace your releases.

❑ Watch for opportunities and trends.

❑ Make the envelope containing your releases the sign of performance.

❑ Razzle-dazzle, a little.

# Media Relations:
## Getting and Maximizing an Interview

While at the Performance Racing Industry Show for those in the motorsports business, the editors of *Performance Racing Industry Magazine*, the people who put on the show, shared their thoughts on publicity. Discussing opportunities for getting motorsports clients quoted in the magazine, they commented, "We're always looking for people to interview, but we'll call someone four or five times and they don't return the call. Then, when the story comes out, they call up and ask why they weren't included." Go figure!

In spite of what Mike Wallace and his *60 Minutes* crowd have taught you to believe, journalists are not out to get you. The media are a prime example of the principle of GIGO: Garbage In, Garbage Out. The stories you read are only as good as the sources the reporter has available. And reporters, even the ones who write for specialty or trade magazines, have to be generalists. They rely on your expertise. They know what brake pads are, for example, but won't understand why your company's are better, unless you tell them. If the reporter can't get you to respond, s/he will keep calling around to your competitors to find someone who will.

## *Lesson One: Return Phone Calls from Reporters*

What could be easier? You don't need to identify the magazines that might be interested in what you have to say. You don't need to figure out which reporter at which magazine covers your area of specialization. You don't need to play telephone tag with that reporter (or, at least not as much). And you don't need to sell your expertise. The reporter has called you. So getting the interview is all the way to Step Five already. It's just a matter of answering the questions and making things clear enough for the reporter to understand what you're saying.

## *Lesson Two: Do It Promptly!*

Reporters are always on a deadline. The chances are very good that when you do talk to the reporter who's called, you'll hear the tapping of computer keys as you speak. If you're lucky, the person has done some advance research, collected your catalog or brochure, visited your Website, read some of your ads (it still makes things easier in working with the trades if your ads appear in the magazine s/he writes for), and now wants to clarify some questions that have come up while writing the piece. Or the editor may have asked for some fact-checking.

On the other hand, you may be in the position of playing professor for someone who has only a vague idea of how race brakes, for example, work, and needs to be able to talk the jargon and report on the latest technology in a way that the readers of the magazine understand.

Whatever the situation, your job is to make it all clear, while putting yourself and your business in the best light. So keep it simple, and make sure you explain why you think what you do is the best way to go — in terms of features and benefits. If you've got the facts to back it up, tell the reporter why your product or service is better than your competitor's. If you don't want to be confrontational about it, just explain why you think your way is best.

If a question comes up that you can't answer, don't be afraid to say, "I don't know." If you don't remember some specific, it's fine to say, "I want to be accurate on that, let me check and get right back to you." Then do. Remember, the article is being written as you speak. If you don't call back to fill in the blank you've left, the entire thought and comment will probably be deleted from the story.

## *Know Your Editor, Audiences, and Media Lists*

The phone isn't ringing and you have a story to tell. How do you make an interview happen? There's quite a bit to it. That is why people can make a career out of media relations. But it's not magic, it's just common sense.

The single biggest mistake you can make in seeking publicity is failing to understand that the currency the media trade in is news. Unless you can convince a reporter or editor that what you're saying is new and different, something their readers will be really interested to know, your effort will appear to be simply self-serving. They'll tell you to go away. Unfortunately, if your news even vaguely resembles news they reported last month, you'll hear, "I'm sorry, we just covered that story." So let's go back to the steps outlined at the beginning of the chapter.

Think of your objective as not just getting an interview, but getting an interview in a specific publication, or category of publications. Looking at your objective this way, it's clear you need to do some research — find out what your options are, and then focus on the one where your story will be news. For example, you're a new hotel and you're trying to generate basic awareness. You want to be noticed by travel editors, local business, real estate and lifestyle editors; meeting, travel agent, corporate travel, and lodging trades; local, associate, and trade "Who's Who" columns; airline in-flight magazines; and the "Personal Business" editors of publications like *Business Week* and *Fortune*.

In this list there are headings for 13 different media lists, each with numerous contacts. For example, the list of full-time travel editors and travel freelancers in the U.S. numbers in the hundreds, including all the members of the Society of American Travel Writers. There are 2,000+ editors and writers interested in news on Websites. Create as many media lists and databases (name, address, phone, fax, and e-mail contact information), in as many formats as you need (labels, e-mail groups). It's much easier to target your editors with appropriate releases if you haven't lumped everyone together on one list. This will save you the embarrassment of sending a personnel announcement to the editor of *Travel & Leisure*. It will also encourage you to craft specific, news-filled releases.

Pick the low-hanging fruit first, as they say. A new hotel, unless it has never-seen-before amenities or services, will be of more interest to the travel, business, and lifestyle editors in your own backyard, and to the various trades, than it will be to a national consumer publication. The importance of your news to a consumer editor grows in direct proportion to how close it is to the publication.

To offer another example: you have a new product or service and you want your potential customers to hear about. First off, nearly every trade publication has New Product blurbs that appear at the back of the book. So research what the publications are and send out your press release and photo. To get an interview, include a letter that says you're available, outlining the key points of your news. While it is less likely that you'll be profiled in the magazine by yourself, it is very likely that the next time the publication explores your subject, the editor will call.

You can help guarantee this will happen if you time your letter to arrive just as the editor is assigning the story. As the folks at the trade magazine, *Performance Racing Industry* suggest, get a copy of the magazine's Editorial Calendar and find out when they're planning a story on your specialty. Three months prior to the issue date, send your letter and then make a phone call to see if there's any interest in what you have to say.

## Know Where and Who, Then Focus on How and When

Who wants to know your news at the publication? A little research will answer the question. The more familiar you are with your customer — the editor or reporter of a particular magazine, in this case — the more likely you are to score bigger. If you want to be quoted in *Performance Racing Industry* or *Travel Weekly*, you should know who's been covering your field. If you don't know, the best route is to start with the names listed as editor-in-chief. They're the ones who ultimately approve or discard a story and will help you shape your news to suit their needs.

To get an interview with your targeted reporter, you need to get his or her attention and sell your news. The best way to do this is to send a letter outlining the highlights, and follow up with a phone call. The better the job you do in the letter of positioning your product, service, or story within its general environment, the better your chances that the reporter will understand that what you're saying is news.

If you say, "XYZ Motorsports announces a new suspension kit" your letter will go to the intern who wades though all the New Products announcements. But if you say, "More and more sports cars enthusiasts are taking their speed events seriously and XYZ Motorsports has designed a new suspension component for the MacPherson-type strut systems the majority of these competitors' cars have. You should take a look at what's happening in this area for the article on Suspensions you have planned for the April issue. I've included some background and the number where I can be reached" the editor will pass it along to the person s/he's assigned to that story. And when you call to follow up, s/he'll tell you who that person is and where s/he can be reached.

Magazines like *Performance Racing Industry* work on two- to three-month lead times, so if you want to be contacted for an April story, send your letter in late January and follow up a week to 10 days later with your phone call. Find out when your local weekly or monthly goes to press, and what is a good day and time to call the reporter. If s/he's on deadline with another story, the worst thing you can do is interrupt with a prospecting call.

## *Maximizing an Interview — Missed and Made Opportunities*

Once you have scheduled an interview, maximize the opportunity. Your interview candidate should be prepared — both mentally and in terms of his or her appearance. Has anyone else noticed how many spokespersons show up for TV interviews in civvies? Here's the perfect opportunity for lengthy on-air exposure for the client's brand and they're in a personal golf shirt, no logo to be found. Some race car drivers maximize this situation by having interview driving suits, lighter-weight, non-Nomex, suits that in many cases have more embroidered logos than the driving suits they wear in the car. Sports networks have carried the idea through by putting their on-air talent in blazers — even drivers' suits for the motorsports reporters — with network-logo-embroidered suits, golf shirts, and jackets. When we were working with Splashdown foul weather gear we made efforts to get the local weather reporters — the ones who were standing out by the freeway in the snowstorm to demonstrate how bad road conditions were — to wear Splashdown gear. We put their logo and ours where it could be seen on a monitor.

So why do PR people, who presumably coordinated the appearance — forget?

PR marketers never underestimate the importance of the uniform, of each team member living up to its standards, of being "on stage" when you wear the company colors in the trade show booth. I'll give you another example of the impact of that uniform on how the brand is perceived.

At the New Hampshire International Speedway a few years ago, a member of Ward Burton's crew was on the phone in the Checkered Flag infield restaurant, which tends to get quite crowded. He was instantly recognizable because he had his full Qualifying Day MBNA uniform on. As we passed, this nice-looking young guy said into the phone, "Just remember, keep your eye on the ball. Play just like you did the other night .... Love you, too, I'll be home soon."

Dad — in the guise of a cutting-edge NASCAR pit crew member, a long way from home — and an absolutely quintessential example of the family values and esprit de corps NASCAR is justly famous for. This guy wasn't put in place by the team's PR person, but he was exemplifying everything MBNA and all the team's other sponsors believe in, while conveying a message about those values to everyone around him.

That's the real magic the PR marketer strives to create. NASCAR's image parade has made fans loyal and sponsors willing to spend huge amounts of marketing dollars to keep fans buying their products and it's a lesson that should not be lost on anyone trying to make an impact. So why no logo on the golf shirt when he's on camera? Missed opportunity, pure and simple.

## Color Notes and Background Insight

Another opportunity missed or made is remembering to supply the editors, analysts, and other second-order opinion-shapers with facts and figures and interesting color notes about your business. It's a continuous process, not a one-time press release distribution; and it must be done in advance. Who knows your business better than you do? Figure out when the high points in your business calendar will come and time your information so the influencers help keep you ahead of the curve. This is a symbiotic relationship — at the same time you are helping them maintain their reputations as trend spotters. Especially for short-term events, you shouldn't save the facts for the day of the event if there's the likelihood that the media will be covering it in depth. At car races you see reporters carrying spiral-bound books full of information on the teams. Do you think your information would get into that spiral-bound volume if you gave it to the track PR people on the afternoon of the race?

Get a press kit, or at least a press release on your participation in the event to the marketing coordinator as soon as you've sent in your entry. Better still, send it with your entry. This holds true for businesses participating in trade shows as well. A professional show manager works the publicity for the event for months before it happens. If s/he can say something specific about one of the exhibitors — product, expertise, what you're presenting at the show — the show gains credibility and customers might even decide to attend an event, specifically to see you! Planning is everything. Be prepared, then follow through.

If you've followed the thinking this far, you'll agree that there's another opportunity that's frequently missed, simply for lack of time and planning. When you draft that press release about your participation in the upcoming trade show or event, think of a call to action. For the race press release, you should be explaining why your team and driver are worth an interview. It's not just that s/he's participating, it's that your driver is coming into the event with a terrific track record, or a plan for turning around one that's mediocre, or a local show car appearance the night before to draw more attention (and sales) to the sponsor.

For a business, your press release should announce a contest centered on the new product you're introducing, or a special guest at the booth, or a special demonstration. Again, the show management will be thrilled to have an exhibitor contributing to their show. Don't be surprised when the managers thank you for supplying coupons, special guests, and press releases. You may find that out of all the exhibitors to whom they had extended the offer of materials distribution and hype, you were the only ones who responded!

Talk about missed opportunities! That attitude not only leaves you in the shadows, it leaves money — cold, hard, cash that might have resulted from the show's greater publicity reach — on the table. Sort of like wearing a plain golf shirt when you've been invited to show your colors on national television.

Publicity is as often about creating news as reporting it. You have to think like a reporter and pick up on what's happening around you that might make a great story or photo op. When you're good at it, the opportunity you have made will include a funny, heartwarming, or exciting moment, a peek into the human side of your company. Made opportunities are the key to building relationships with the on-air media and reporters who cover your circuit or business, too. Their job is to tell the story, but there's no way they can cover all the ground they're assigned. Some media watchers estimate that over 80 percent of the information you hear or read is PR-generated. So get out there. Give them a good story to tell and, like the frog who became a prince, you'll be transformed from flack to resource.

## Pet Peeves

It would seem obvious that it doesn't help your media relations cause to aggravate the editor, yet this is what some PR people do all the time — to hear the editors speak.

No matter what the industry, editors and reporters seem to share the same pet peeves. One of the best summaries I've heard is the voice mail message on *Boston Globe* Travel Editor, Jerry Morris' extension. He says, "If it's Monday, I'm not here. If you're calling to ask about a press release, I have it. If you're calling about freelance stories, yes, we accept them. Mail it to me at *The Globe.* If you've lasted this long and still want to leave a message, do so at the tone."

With all the new ways there are to communicate — snail mail, voice mail, and e-mail — there are even more ways to alienate your customer, the editor. So here are some of the Pet Peeves of Media Relations:

- People who don't bother to find out anything about my publication before sending me press releases. More trees are wasted on the misguided assumption that sending the same press release to every name on the masthead is better than targeting the single person who can most use your news. Sending a press release that will be outdated by the time the publication appears and sending product information to technical journals are also high on the annoyance list.

- People who are sloppy about addresses. If all you have is "Editor" above the address on your mailing list, save the postage. If you have a name, make sure it's spelled correctly and is printed tidily on the envelope. Sloppy mailings suggest your content is sloppy, too.

- E-mails with attachments. One editor commented, "Like I have time to go find them and keep the attachment correlated with the message. Learn how to copy and paste!" The syntax of e-mail is short and to the point. You're putting up a billboard, not writing the great American novel.

- People who waste time. No one has time to be wasted. Your job is to sell your story, so prepare your most-convincing pitch before you pick up the phone. Don't read your pitch, wander around your subject, or put anything else in the way of getting to the point. If you can't talk about your subject on the fly, you'd better rehearse some more. It is often useful to send a brief outline of your selling points in advance, in a pitch letter. Nine times out of 10, the editor will not remember having seen it, but the exercise organizes your thoughts so you can talk on your feet.

Your job is to be a resource to editors and reporters. To be a professional resource, you need to thoroughly understand your product. You should be able to think of more story angles and nuances than the reporters, and you should never forget that your job is to be a facilitator, not a flack. Never put yourself in the position of being, "one of those people who call me on the phone and tell me how to run my publication. Telling me what I should or must not do is not a good way to get me to do anything."

## The Care and Feeding of On-Site Media
### Press Conferences and Crisis Communications

In the world of instantaneous transmission of information, the press conference, surprisingly, has lost favor, except in crisis communications situations. Generally, if you call a press conference, no one will come — unless your company and its news is globally important. Earth-shaking news, including such crises as hotel fires, strikes, hurricane effects, plane crashes and the like require not just a press conference, but a series of them. See Appendix II, the Hotel Crisis Communications Plan, for an example of the logistics — setting up a media center separate from the command center, how and when information should be presented, and other details. Everyone who has been through a crisis communications situation agrees that if you recognize the media's need for information by providing regular updates containing credible detail, they will treat you fairly. Advance planning and proactivity are the secrets. The government of The Islands of The Bahamas uses a crisis communications plan developed by BSMG in New York, and Irma S. Mann, Strategic Marketing, Inc. in Boston to give both the media and travel agents information about developing stories such as impending hurricanes. The agencies use emergency fax broadcasts to lists of broadcast meteorologists, news outlets, their consumer 800-number, and travel agencies, to keep them informed. The advisories come directly from the Bahamian government.

## Wire Service and Internet Release Distribution

Soft news, which used to be announced via a press conference, is now announced via wire service and Internet release such as BusinessWire, PR Newswire, and WebPromote. All of these have their own Websites and are a good source for more information on electronic press release distribution. Soft news can get local media attention if you create a photo opportunity. The opening of a new 210-room hotel in Boston was certainly not going to make the noon news. By creating the first-ever, real-time, hotel ribbon-cutting in cyberspace, with the technical assistance of the MIT Media Lab Wearable Computers project, the University Park Hotel at MIT opened in the presence of TV camera crews and a reporter from the Associated Press.

## Media Advisories

When trying to attract the broadcast media and the major daily newspapers, your best approach is to send out a Media Advisory. This one-page sheet literally calls out Who, What, Where, When, and Why, in bare-bones details and in big type. Before sending out this Advisory, call the assignment desks and describe the event in two sentences. Then ask if they'd like you to fax over a "Who, What, Why" advisory with the details. In one phone call you've pitched the story and discovered the chances that the news desk will assign someone. Don't be surprised if the editor you talk to on Thursday, who seems really excited, is not there come Monday morning, the day of your event or that the new guy couldn't care less.

## Vertical Niche Press Conferences

The one instance where press conferences are still held are niche arenas: trade shows and sport events. This may be because the media are gathered and focused on one subject. Companies almost always stage new product releases during their industry's major trade shows, for this reason. PR people for race teams and other sports entities can generally use the track or stadium media centers to good effect — to announce a new sponsor, coach or player.

## Media Briefings

In place of press conferences, backgrounder sessions have become standard operating procedure. The White House Press Conference is really an example of a media briefing. So is the Analyst Session that companies announcing an IPO (independent public offering) arrange. At the three major hotel investor conferences (UCLA, NYU, and Morris Laskey's Conference) these sessions give industry analysts and trade editors for hospitality and real estate a chance to interview the principals. Arranging such a briefing for your company president can also be effective. Whether you're inviting *Commercial Property News, Hotel Business, Northeast Real Estate News,* and the *New York Times* to a breakfast session in Manhattan, or your local business editor for coffee in the local café, these sessions are low key, question and answer opportunities designed to achieve the goal of establishing a relationship. Do your homework. Be candid and friendly, and you'll have a media friend when you've got news to tell.

## *Press Trips*

In the travel and tourism industries, you have the luxury of being able to arrange press trips to visit your hotel or attraction. You can conduct a press trip in virtually any industry, as long as you give the invitees something to look at that is worth all the time they invest in the process.

For a travel destination, or a specific hotel or attraction, it is important to offer a representative smorgasbord — while not expecting what some participants call a forced march. It is unrealistic for the typical hotel to expect senior travel editors to travel any distance simply to inspect a new property, no matter how nice or unusual. From reading their stories you will know that the typical travel editor spends more time talking about what there is to do right outside the hotel door, than on the guestroom décor. So plan the press trip accordingly. Showcase the best of your location, preferably within a context that reinforces the positioning of your hotel. If you're doing a press trip for the Omni Parker House, the oldest continuously-operating hotel in America, you include a tour of the Freedom Trail which links Revolutionary War-era historic sites in Boston. When you're showcasing the University Park Hotel at MIT, you tour MIT, Harvard, Central Square, and the Museum of Science.

Keep the group small so the logistics are manageable. Provide background information by mail, in advance, so the writers can prepare themselves for the trip and not have to lug press kits home with them. Send the travel specifics, including phone numbers where they can be reached. Cover everything but personal expenses, except in those situations where the publication insists they pay their own way. This was a major ethical controversy a while ago, as some papers felt their integrity would be questioned if a reporter delivered a favorable review of a place that had paid his or her way. The reporters felt their own integrity was being called into question. This is merely a heads-up for you to ask those you invite whether their publications have policies on what the host may offer.

To sum up:

- If you do a good enough job in selling your story idea, recognizing the needs of the editor, reporter, and their magazine and if you clearly explain not only what you do, but what's happening in your field, the chances are very good that the reporter will call you again.
- Media relations is like any other selling situation. Treat your news as the product, the editor or reporter as the customer. Understand what s/he needs before pushing the sale, and present the features and benefits of your news (as well as your product or service) to close the deal. If your customer is pleased with what s/he bought, s/he'll be back for more.

## *Media Relations Checklist*

1. If you do a good enough job, the reporter will call you again.
   - ❏ Do you understand your product?
   - ❏ Can you sum up the news angle succinctly?
   - ❏ Can you sell your story idea?
   - ❏ Do you recognize the needs of the editor, reporter, publication?
   - ❏ Can you explain what you do in context of what's happening in your field?

2. Getting an interview is making a sale.
   - ❏ Can you define your news product?
   - ❏ Do you treat your media contact as a customer?
   - ❏ Do you understand their needs before pushing the sale?
   - ❏ Can you distinguish the features and benefits of your news?

3. Avoid these pet peeves.
   - ❏ Do you do blanket mailings, or send the right news to the right publications?
   - ❏ Do you call to ask if the editor has received your release?
   - ❏ Do you call to ask if your e-mail was received?

❏ Are you unable to articulate your story idea?

❏ Do you offer information too late?

❏ Do you forget to include contact and price information?

❏ Do you call West Coast editors at 9 A.M. EST?

❏ Do you tell editors how they should run their publications?

4. The care and feeding of on-site media:

❏ Do you have a crisis communications plan?

❏ Do you create Media Advisories for photo opportunities?

❏ Do you leverage media attendance at trade shows and other events?

❏ Do you schedule backgrounder sessions for editors to meet your executives?

❏ Do you make press trips worth the participants' time?

# 7

# Evaluating Sponsorship Opportunities

An article in the *Wall Street Journal* a while ago led off with the head-line, "It needn't always cost a bundle to get consumers to notice unknown brands." It talked about the effectiveness of exposure through product placement, citing the example of little Franklin Sports Industries, that no one had heard of in 1980, even though it was selling to some of the same school and institutional accounts as the sporting goods giant, Spaulding.

When Philadelphia Phillies star Mike Schmidt signed on with Franklin as a consultant, he told them that batters' gloves were a potential specialty area. So Franklin designed a special glove, put its logo in inch-high let-ters on the back, and started giving them out to major league players. The name showed up all over the media, from television to the cover of *Sports Illustrated* ... and established Franklin's credibility as a major league player, while driving annual sales from $15 to $65 million.

## Generating Awareness and Credibility

Sponsorship for any company depends on basically the same idea. Get your name, and preferably your product, into an arena that lends credibil-ity-by-association to your identity and story. Played smart, sponsorship provides some of the biggest bang for the buck. And the bucks are getting bigger all the time because sponsored events and properties know this. In motorsports and professional skating, for example, the value of every flat surface (as well as some you wouldn't expect, like the rear axle) is calculated to the nearest square inch. In most arenas you need to be creative with your associated marketing to get the most out of your sponsorship dollars.

At the same time, there are many events out there looking for sponsors who either don't understand what you need to feel you've earned a return on your investment, or don't deliver what they promise. You need a formal measurement standard to evaluate opportunities and results.

Promotions — where you get free publicity and visibility in high traffic areas in exchange for a little cash and going a little out of your way — are the answer. Sponsorships are an especially effective means for grabbing your moment in the spotlight because most of the event planning is done by someone else. Unlike a special event such as an open house when you are a sponsor, all you do is worry about your act, not the refreshments unless, of course, you're a food and beverage vendor or distributor.

The key is smart marketing. What do you expect to accomplish?

When Splashdown USA decided to go up against the big companies in the foul weather gear industry, we helped them make a choice like Franklin Sporting Goods. They decided to award their unique waterproof jackets to the winners of national sailing regattas, thus giving Splashdown USA a guaranteed position in the spotlight, in front of hundreds of racing sailors (their target audience) in key markets on both coasts. This gave their brand instant credibility, because suddenly the stars of the sport were walking around in their Splashdown award jackets, which it turned out they preferred over what they had been wearing. One national champion told the President of the company that he had stacks of jackets and foul weather gear in the closet and the first one he always reached for was his Splashdown.

## Ten Questions to Ask Before Getting Involved

To gain the same recognition for your brand, product, or business, ask yourself the following questions the next time someone asks you to help sponsor an event. If the answers you get aren't good enough, this process helps you explain to the persistent sponsor-seeker why it just doesn't make sense for you right now.

## Audience

1. Does the audience for the event match my target customer — or will there be more people there who aren't my customer than people who are?

## Barter

2. Is there an opportunity for me to provide product or services instead of paying cash for my sponsorship? The best event to sponsor is one that showcases your product, either as an award or as one of the event elements like refreshments or computer scoring.

## Sales

3. Can I set up shop and actually sell product to customers at the event — or at least distribute information and/or samples? While many private clubs or charitable organizations carefully monitor commercial pursuits on their grounds, more and more of them understand the value sponsors add to their events. If you can only hand out catalogs, make sure you give the people who attend the event an incentive to find your store or product — a discount coupon works well for this. If you can't even put catalogs in the goody bags, why are you sponsoring this event?

## Sales Potential

4. If you're making a major commitment of product — for example, all the beer, jackets for the winners of each class, all the landscaping — is the audience for the event likely to match the cost of this outlay with future purchases? If the answer is probably not, then you should ask yourself whether your association with this event is high-profile enough to raise the status, awareness, and credibility of your business.

## Exclusivity

5. Is my sponsorship of this event an exclusive in my niche? Am I the only clothing company, landscaper or beer company? One of the benefits of sponsorship is saturation of the audience with your name. Repetition over an afternoon or weekend (to say nothing of the weeks leading up to the event) is key. If you own the category, people will remember more about your product than if they're trying to sort out whether it was your stuff they really liked or the other guy's.

## Event Management

6. How well organized is this event? Is it an annual tradition, with a committee for everything? Or is it hard to get your questions

answered? By being a sponsor, you tie your identity to the event; that's where the added credibility comes from. If the event is a disaster, you run the risk of going down with the ship, too. The more responsive, proactive, and creative the event organization is, the more you're likely to benefit from it. The events that inevitably fizzle are the ones that should have raised serious questions in your mind at the first sponsors' meeting. Keep in mind the added value of an annual event. You don't have to ask yourself these questions all over again next year; and people who liked it this year will be looking for you and your product next year.

## Event Promotion and Publicity

7. A corollary to Question 6: what's the publicity plan for the event? How are the organizers planning to generate the attendance they're promising? What about your own publicity? Are there ways you can add to the gate by putting up posters, giving (and mailing) out flyers, going on the local cable TV station to plug the whole event as well as your participation?

## Promotional Tie-Ins

8. Does sponsorship of this event give you tie-ins for promotions with your customers, vendors, and employees? Ways to say thanks to your best accounts? Any time you can move the barricades for the people you wish would do the same for you, you're earning goodwill returns on your sponsorship investment.

## Measurability

9. Will you know if your sponsorship was worth it when you're done? Measurability is the element that is so often missing — and is one of the biggest reasons the sponsors of a given event change so often. Sales receipts from product sold at the event, press clips with your company's name and pictures with your logo, publicity pictures for your future use of event celebrities holding or wearing your product (and their permissions to use the photos in your publicity), and event collateral with your logo — these all have value. The measures don't have to be revenues, although increasing revenues is always the ultimate goal of sponsorship. Just be sure there's some tangible evidence that you can count up when you're done.

## Partnership Marketing

10. Is there the opportunity to build valuable long-term relationships — with other sponsors, with the individuals who are organizing the

event, with the event itself? And will my commitment to this sponsorship be a plus to my customers? NASCAR fans report they are 65 percent more likely to choose a product offered by a company that sponsors a NASCAR team than a product from a company that doesn't sponsor, when given the choice. People like their suppliers to support the things they like.

## *Estimating Your Chance for Success*

The bottom line is the same whether you don't know if you've gotten what you paid for or if you didn't get what you paid for. For this good business reason, you should sit down with a piece of paper and actually write down your answers to these questions each time a sponsorship opportunity comes up. Give each item one to 10 points, then add up the total. As there are 10 categories, the total potential is 100 points. You then also rank the categories in importance, from a low of one to a high of 10. By factoring the potential of the event times the importance of that category, you get a value which prevents you from getting involved in events that aren't going to produce the results you want and need. First, multiply your importance rating by 10 in each category, adding the products. You get the total potential, in points which you seek in any sponsorship opportunity. Then multiply the rating by the potential the event you're considering offers and add the sums. Divide this number by the ideal number you got in the first calculations and that score is your chance, in percentage, of being successful in your sponsorship.

For example, Splashdown was invited to sponsor the Gold Cup in Bermuda, a sailing regatta pitting the world's top sailors with Olympic and America's Cup credentials against each other. Figure 7.1 shows how sponsorship opportunities were rated. Figure 7.2 shows how the Gold Cup event rated.

Therefore, Splashdown's chance of success from the sponsorship was 95 percent. The retailer in Bermuda subsequently became the largest single account for the company that year, and Splashdown continued to see sailors and sailing judges in their gear at races all over the globe.

If the opportunity doesn't pan out on paper, either ask more questions (of the event and of your involvement) — or don't get involved. It is always possible that a particular event just isn't a good match for you.

After the event is over and you've collected all your results, sit down with the pad of paper again and see if everything went as you imagined it would, and score the results.

## Figure 7.1: Splashdown USA's Ideal Sponsorship

| | | |
|---|---|---|
| Audience | 10 x 10 | Targets those who wear foul weather gear. |
| Trade | 10 x 10 | Product instead of cash was always sponsorship basis. |
| Sales | 10 x 5 | On-site sales were often a hassle. |
| Future Sales | 10 x 10 | Return on investment through retail sales was paramount. |
| Exclusivity | 10 x 10 | Splashdown's most important sponsorship criterion. |
| Management | 10 x 7 | Less a critical component to the sponsor. |
| Event promotion | 10 x 10 | Sponsorship used to generate brand awareness. |
| Promotions | 10 x 7 | Nice to have, but not critical. |
| Measures | 10 x 10 | Every sponsorship had a measurement. |
| Partners | 10 x 10 | This aspect produced instant credibility by association. |
| TOTAL | 890 Points in Ideal Event. | |

Put a cash value on what you invested as the sponsor, then track the sales or referrals or benefits you get out of it — as people bring in the coupons you handed out and as new clients tell you they learned of your business through the event. If you're pleased with the tally, this sponsorship worked for you! Means a whole lot more than another ad in the program book, doesn't it?

## *Leveraging Sponsorship Opportunities*

Sponsorship is still hard to come by at least in part because some teams who have sponsors don't do enough to promote the name and products when they are in front of the public. Each team — and the businesses who back them — needs to do more subtle merchandising and promotion. To give you some ideas and some practical suggestions, let's look at some examples from racetracks around New England. Whether you're a

## Figure 7.2: Actual Gold Cup Sponsorship Rating

| | | |
|---|---|---|
| Audience | 10 x 10 | The top sailors in the world participated. |
| Trade | 10 x 10 | The $50,000 sponsorship was executed in product-only. |
| Sales | 5 x 0 | No direct selling at the event. |
| Future Sales | 10 x 10 | Event supported the new retail account in Bermuda. |
| Exclusivity | 10 x 10 | Splashdown was the Gold Cup Official Foul Weather Gear. |
| Management | 10 x 7 | Evaluation of the organizers. |
| Promotion | 10 x 10 | Event was televised by ESPN. |
| Opportunity | 7 x 5 | Nice event to bring the manufacturer's Director to. |
| Measures | 10 x 10 | Sales from the Bermuda account; PR from gear wearers. |
| Partners | 10 x 10 | Splashdown joined Mumm, Continental Airlines, Wedgewood. |
| TOTAL | 845 out of 890 = 95%. | |

sponsored team or a motorsports business sponsoring either a team or a race, these are some things you can do to maximize your opportunity:

## Branding the Event

NAPA Auto Parts did a great job at the races they sponsored at Thompson International Speedway in Connecticut. They used billboards at the track and flyers in advance with the company logo. They had a pre-race parade of NAPA trucks complete with their signature caps, and they had a plane over the racetrack towing a banner wishing good luck to Stub Fadden, the Busch North veteran who drove the #16 NAPA car. One exchange could have been handled differently. As the parade lap trucks were lining up to go onto the track, officials told the exhibitors that the children aboard would not be allowed on the track, due to insurance reasons. In the interest of the goodwill you're trying to get with any PR event, the rules at Thompson should have been made clear farther in advance, rather than disappointing the children and the NAPA-associated truck drivers who thought they'd give the kids an extra treat. Plan every eventuality in advance. Don't assume you can do something. Ask — it's better to find out before the last minute so you can make a substitution.

## Employee Hospitality

One of the best showings of sponsor employees comes at the Stanley 150 at New Hampshire International Speedway (NHIS). Stanley — based in Connecticut, a two-hour drive from NHIS — seemed to have hundreds of Team Stanley supporters in attendance. They were enthusiastic fans, judging not only from their cheers in the stands but also from the fact that they trooped back to Loudon a month later, after the original race was postponed due to rain. How could you tell so much about them? They were wearing bright yellow (corporate colors) Stanley hats, carrying Stanley bags, and wearing Stanley shirts or rain ponchos. You could see them in the stands from the garages because they all sat together in a Stanley-yellow group. Plus they overran the garages on their VIP tour.

If you're going to sponsor a car, you should be giving your customers and employees access to the very-desirable perk of spending an afternoon or evening at the track. If you're going to provide the access — and have those guests feel as if they're part of the race team you spend your marketing money on — you should give them something to identify with and to be identified by. Bigger companies with every logoed item you can imagine have an easier time, assuming they plan ahead, ordering shirts, visors, or baseball caps with the team colors. Given the proliferation of companies that produce promotional items, any business can get hats or T-shirts or visors printed; and by doing so, you: 1) give your guests a value-added souvenir; 2) spread your advertising and sponsorship message at the race and whenever your guest wears his or her shirt or hat; and 3) start thinking about the other ways you can leverage your marketing investment at the race event with enough lead time (shirt orders take four to six weeks) to make things happen! One other comment about spreading your advertising message — everyone involved in the sport of motor racing understands the importance of sponsors. When your employees or customers walk through the infield or garages all wearing your company shirt or visor, they are immediately identifiable as people who should be treated as VIP's by all the teams. The drivers try to be accessible to anyone who wants an autograph. But it's human nature for them to pay special attention to the guests of sponsors.

## Identity

It always seems that the teams who have the sharpest-looking uniforms, and the best sponsor graphics on their cars also always have a banner for the garage area and pitwall. At tracks where the team hauler is the garage, there's the benefit of the side of the truck. A number of teams also have portable shelters, with the sponsor's name on the sides. But only a handful of teams have weatherproof banners, deployed as a regular part of setting up shop. Some additional opportunities for sponsor logos currently in use on the Busch North circuit: folding director's chairs in the sponsor color, logo embroidered on the back, flags, and color-coordinated gear bags.

## National Sponsorship Tie-Ins

When a local event brings in the national teams — the Watkins Glen and NHIS weekends where Busch North was the featured support race for Winston Cup, for example — it should be obvious that you want to match up your local effort with what the national sponsor is doing. The GenWall Motorventures Busch North team, that had just picked up sponsorship from the Ford Quality Care and Ford Customer Service Divisions, joined Dale Jarrett and his Quality Care team in the Ford Motor Company hospitality tent for an autograph session. The GenWall Ford Quality Care Thunderbird showcar — because it was more readily available — was the showcar on display all weekend.

On the subject of autograph sessions — they're a great extra reminder of the sponsorship because there's usually a PA announcement that your driver will be signing autographs at whatever time and place.

To get the most out of your sponsorship dollar, take advantage of every opportunity. As you'll read in the next chapter on special events, you should plan your sponsored event to mesh with what's happening in your business. If you're introducing a new product or new location, build an incentive into your announcement: "See the [new product] and register to win race tickets and meet the [company name] team." If there's a new product, put it on display at the racetrack and offer samples, coupons, or flyers to race fans and the teams in the garages.

Match your customer program with an employee incentive and/or team-building program. Order the shirts or hats and make sure the team gets a block of tickets for you. If you have the option, choose your race on the basis of additional potential. Obviously if you're sponsoring a particular race, like the NAPA 150, that's the one you'll build everything else around. Connect with your Winston Cup team when they're making a stop at your local track. Make sure your driver is also signing autographs for the public during the event, in order to get that extra PA benefit, as well as providing the perfect photo opportunity for the picture you'll send to the local newspaper and racing press as a follow-up to the weekend. Put your logo on everything you can think of, so everyone attending the race, as well as everyone in the pit area, sees your visible support for the sport all weekend long.

Sponsorship is not about someone giving away money to let its team go play with race cars. Sponsorship is a way of investing marketing dollars around a common theme so that you can translate race fans' legendary loyalty to motorsports sponsors into brand loyalty and sales. The fans need to be reminded of your sponsorship on and off the track to reap the benefit of increased sales. If you're not doing these things, you're leaving money on the table.

## *Evaluating Sponsorship Form*

| |
|---|
| Audience |
| Trade |
| Sales |
| Future Sales |
| Exclusivity |
| Management |
| Promotion |
| Opportunity |
| Measures |
| Partners |
| TOTAL |

# 8

# *Special Events that Produce*

There's a huge debate constantly raging in the boating industry. See if this sounds familiar. It seems fewer Americans now consider themselves boaters than a decade ago. The indicators are that the downward spiral is a trend that is continuing, even as more people are entering what the industry calls prime boat-owning age, (read those ubiquitous baby boomers).

At the same time, those involved in motorsports on the local scale are trying to explain why fans are drifting away from local racing and why so many short tracks have closed. Some think that sponsors are being put ahead of racing and the interests of the race fans because the tracks and the promoters aren't generating the support racers need to put their cars on the racetrack. In other words, the promoters have forgotten the basic goal in producing an event: getting people to show up! It seems promoters have to roll up their sleeves and go to work. The conclusion from the marine retailers was much the same.

If everyone is going to turn to the promotions and PR people as the saviors of our respective sports, what are promoters supposed to do?

## Who Are You?

Focus is critical and the basic step in focusing is deciding who you are. For any event or event series, whether it's a car racing series or a summer theater, the decision must be: are we going to step up to full-blown, full-time, professional marketing and sales promotion, or are we going to stay the way we are?

For a local, small series just getting off the ground, or a championship that has to stay part-time because the participants just don't have enough time or money to perform as anything but amateurs, "the way things are" is fine.

For the series that wants to generate enough income to make the organizational improvements it needs, swing more clout with individual venues and their promoters, and keep the interest of the fans at the forefront, "the way things are" isn't good enough.

Once the governing body or promoter has accepted the responsibility to grow a series or an event to its next stage, the rest is almost easy, because tried and true approaches to PR and sales promotion *work*. Easy doesn't mean that it's less work to promote a series than it is to sit there and let people come to you. It is a lot of work, but one of the great impediments to success is fear, which results in hesitancy, then failure. If you don't ask, the automatic answer is no.

## Who Is the Customer?

Once you've made the decision as a promoter that you're going to promote and sell the best product that's out there, you take completely logical steps to realize that ambition and you come to the next promotional basic: define who is your customer and how does s/he think? What attracts your customer? What will it take to make your product deliver satisfaction to the customer? How do you increase sales? Note the sequence. Put increasing sales first and you won't get the first two done — and you won't increase sales, either.

You can see that if you don't answer the first two basic questions, you won't be in the place you need to be in your thinking to answer the third successfully. This seems to be why so many event productions fail. They fail their customers! They're letting the baggage of the production get in the way of the fans in just the same way as if they built a wall around the event that no one could see over!

When you start thinking in terms of generating attendance, you do things like eliminate the need for a family to find a babysitter — you hold family nights where kids under 12 get in free. You make racing enticing like the Hooter's Cup has done — offer huge purses and then show the races on closed circuit TV in nearby restaurants, thereby generating the additional revenue that helps pay for those purses. Clean up your act literally (restrooms and concession stands) as well as eliminating the special interests that make the event dull and the attendance experience unpleasant. You widen the appeal of live performance to more groups that sponsors want to reach. Maybe go after television exposure for your special event. Don't think you're too small for TV. If community access cable can cover the local high school football game, they can cover your event. "If they can watch it on TV they won't come to my production"? Wrong! Remember, one of your biggest competitors for fans' interest is the 200 channels of satellite and cable television and when they see a local performance on television, live events are more attractive, draw more sponsor support, and more awareness of the art as an entertainment alternative.

All of these approaches look at productions from the point of view of the customer — the fan — and deliver the message that there is value in live performances, for the entertainment dollar spent. The role of PR is nothing more than this: convincing people yours is better than theirs.

## The Role of the Advance Person

Once you've created a package of ideas that could attract your audience, then: Tell Them.

In the early days of the small traveling circuses, there was a person whose sole job was to travel ahead of the circus, putting up the posters, running the newspaper ads, and handing out the handbills to make sure that when the circus came to town there was a crowd there to meet it. If a circus, likely the most different, most exciting, most compelling event to happen in a given small town in months, needed an advance person, what makes you think your production — that competes with thousands of entertainment alternatives — each backed with millions of dollars of professional talent, and the most sophisticated production values — doesn't?

Racecars still draw crowds. That's why Winston Cup sponsors spend the money they do on showcars. The sad truth is that many other types of events won't draw a crowd unless you make it exotic. "Exotic" is having Bill Elliott's racecar in front of the local McDonald's. That is exotic because it's unexpected, glamorous, and different to the usual customers at that McDonald's. They aren't accustomed to seeing a racecar there and the car as a focal point makes it easy for them to imagine the excitement. It gets their attention. Sticking with our circus analogy — why do you think the circus parade was invented? Because people would follow a clown and an elephant down Main Street to see where they were going, and maybe buy a ticket to go inside the Big Top for the show!

Why do people who have a tame tiger, so to speak, have empty stands when they let the tiger out to do its thing. Perhaps nobody knows the tiger is there. Once you follow the clown and the elephant, it's hard not to stay for the show.

How do you tell them? Consider every venue in your series' schedule, a special event, to be treated accordingly. Identify the audiences for the event. Send invitations via every medium you can manage: posters, flyers, handbills, press releases, newspaper, radio, and TV ads, or elephants. Work the publicity hard. Form marketing partnerships with local chambers of commerce, stage autograph sessions, radio station remote broadcasts, and prize drawings. These work so well that your audience is happy even if the production is sold out and they can't get tickets! Keep your name — and the excitement of your event — out where the fans can see.

## *Be Professional*

Hone your talents and your results. Get better and better. Be more and more professional. Deliver more and more value to your fans and to your performers. You're still competing with the production values of the television industry for your customer's dollar and you have to make your show more entertaining, more worth his or her time and dollar, to keep the crowds coming. Be professional in your media efforts. Learn how to write a press release and how to build relationships with reporters. Teach your local sports editor — and lifestyle editor — why your event is something their readers care about. Keep the focus on who you are; build on the excitement, and they will come.

People like to be where the action is. Live audiences, by definition, get exactly that. At a time when TV coverage of motorsports is creating a phenomenon that even *Forbes* and *Nightline* notice, a racetrack or a racing series should be a gold-mine for its owners. It's time to make "promoter" a positive word.

# *The How-To's*

Some say that if you put a race car down in an empty field, it will draw a crowd. That's because race cars embody the inherent excitement and appeal of racing. That's the basic idea behind offering a special event. But drawing a crowd isn't always enough of a goal. There's always the risk of putting extra effort into a special event and getting minimal return — the old, "what if you gave a party and nobody came?" Therefore, we need to look at the what's and why's of special events in order to reduce the risks and maximize the results. Some details to consider:

- Drawing people to your event.
- Inviting those you want to attend.
- Taking advantage of all the peripheral ways you can leverage your special event for even more exposure, sales, and publicity.
- Building in a measure of results.

## What's the Occasion?

What does the art of attracting attention involve? Understanding what attracts people helps you decide what you will produce as your special event.

Presumably, you have something you want to say. If you're a race team planning a show car appearance at your sponsor's local franchise location, what you want to say is: "Look at this race car in its [franchisee] paint job! Isn't it terrific that the sponsor supports racing — terrific enough that you should buy the product?"

In this case, all you really need to do is what you do best — be a race team. Position your driver and crew as the stars of the show. Dress them in full race costume. Let people take pictures of themselves acting out their fantasy of being behind the wheel of a race car. Sign autographs. Smile and show how much fun you're having because your sponsor supports fun stuff.

If you're a consultant on Internet marketing, what you want to say is, "We're the experts in helping you set up a Website that produces results." Your special event might be an open house to showcase new software, or an appearance at a trade show, or a seminar at the Advertising Club meeting where you offer expertise on your specialty.

In each case, because what you want to communicate is expertise, you have to produce an event that demonstrates expertise and puts your experts on display. In the case of an open house for a new product, you want to get the factory rep for the product in to offer a brief talk on whatever it is. The more show and tell the talk has, demonstrating sites where the software was used to create in real time on the 'Net, or previewing a new page for a hot site to your audience, the more "expert" connotations rub off on your shop.

Of course if you're the manufacturer of the product, you want to schedule a series of these open house events with every distributor you have, or on a regional basis. As the manufacturer, you can either present an open house for customers in conjunction with your retail owners, or you can present a dealers' day and include more technical training on how to sell your product — and on selling or merchandising in general.

## Content

The better your relationship with the proposed audience for your special event, the longer you can make your presentation. If you're introducing a new product to a wide customer base, keep it short — 15 minutes of sales pitch. Then make yourself available to answer questions one-on-one with the people who want to talk technical. There will always be some "hangers-on" who want to listen and learn but don't want to feel pressured by their lack of knowledge or the sales pitch they suppose you will give them. Encourage them — an educated customer is your best customer. If you're a manufacturer and plan to invite your retail accounts to an open house at the factory, you can schedule a half, even a full day, if you have enough going on to keep things interesting and if you already have a good working relationship with that field team.

An example of this is Saturn. They convinced a reported 40,000 people to spend a weekend at the plant in Spring Hill, Tennessee. Sure they had fun things to do — a tour of the factory, a barbecue in the rain — but that mother of all PR special events worked so well because Saturn has worked at developing an ongoing relationship with its customers. On the other hand, an exhibitor at the Performance Racing Industry Show produced an excellent seminar — there were expert speakers, live action videos, professionally packaged information kits, and refreshments. But the turn-out was low, at least in part because the session was advertised to be 2½ hours long and the audience was too unfamiliar with the company to commit that kind of time. Catch-22: the more you have to say about your business, the less time you have to say it the first time around. See the chapter on customer databases for suggestions on building those relationships and keeping track of the information you learn.

## Refreshments

Feed them and they will come. Always offer refreshments. Think of your special event as a party. What's a party without food and drink? Keep it appropriate — in terms of cost, clean-up, and conscience. A bowl of hard candies on the counter — and maybe the offer of a coffee or soft drink — at the shop and at the show is sufficient. Bowls of pretzels or chips and maybe some salsa and cookies is the route for an open house. A buffet lunch of cold cuts is the usual drill for a day-long session.

## Gifts

Giveaways are good. Your appearance should always be accompanied by a supply of brochures plus hats or T-shirts if you have them to award as prizes in the store or to give to employees. Hold a drawing for one customer to win the product your open house is showcasing and see if the manufacturer has any handouts — both printed information and promotional items (trial software disks, or mouse pads). Give those who attend some tangible reward for coming.

## Selecting an Audience

When you have enough of an idea of what you'd like to communicate, you must decide whom you want to get the message. In the case of a race team show car appearance, you want potential customers for your sponsor's product to feel good about the sponsor. So you need to let current customers know you're coming and tell people who might be good customers that there's a reason to come down to the store or franchise next Thursday evening — you'll make it worth their while.

If you're the Internet consultant, you want your customers — especially those you know would be excited by the possibilities that the new software offers — to know that you're planning an event they might want to check out. If you're a new business, you want to reach all the potential customers in the area: those people you knew were "out there" when you selected your business location and put your ad in the yellow pages. If you're Saturn, you invite everyone who bought a Saturn car in the last five years.

How do you invite those audiences to your event? You send out invitations! It really is that basic; and you can see how planning a special event is not so difficult if you plan out the steps logically. The most effective special events are never based on the premise of build it, and they will come. Far from it! They're artful ways of leading people who have vested interests in hearing what you have to say to the fountain and making sure they enjoy themselves while they drink it all in.

## Invitations and Publicity

Invitations can take the form of a broad range of media, from the company memo to its retail distributors, to a six-foot vinyl banner hung out in front of the racecar sponsor's restaurant saying, "[Your] Race Team! Here Thursday Night! Driver Autographs! Free Prizes!" Match the medium not only to the message but to the most effective way of reaching the audience you have identified for your show.

Use as many different media as you can afford, based on: 1) the challenge in reaching your target audience with your message; and 2) the sales return you expect to get from your effort. The closer you are to those customers you want to invite, the less you have to work at inviting them. Some customers may only need a verbal invitation. Customers you don't see every day should get a flyer, preferably in invitation format, in the mail. New customers who walk into the store should see a copy of the flyer set up in a counter stand display, with take-home copies next to it and your verbal invitation to reinforce the point.

An ad in your local trade paper or daily news and a press release announcing the event mailed to all of the local business pubs and professional organizations spread the news farther and improve the chances of your event's success. Don't forget time, date, and place!

Announcements and invitations all require advance planning if they are to "register" in time to do your event's attendance any good. The advance notice you require depends, again, on how close you are to your intended audience. The bigger the event, the more notice you need. If you're planning a birthday party with friends when you're all at the ski lodge, they need less notice than when you're planning a wedding. You need enough advance notice to get a clear date on their calendars and enough time to remind people who want to come but forgot to write it down the first time.

A month or even two may be needed for a major event like a manufacturer's day — or to get hold of members of a club that meets only once a month. Ten days should be enough to announce a show car appearance at the local Burger King. The show car schedule generally takes much more advance planning to coordinate the team, its racing demands, and all the different stops your sponsor would like you to include.

Most press release calendar listings take two to three weeks of advance notice. Be aware that some calendar listings include only community and charity events. If you can tie such a message into your special event and still accomplish what you set out to do, you'll have more help with publicity pick-up than if your event is an obviously self-serving one. Newspaper ads in weekly trade and community papers are due at least a week, often two to three weeks before the publication date of the issue you want to be in.

In general, then, a month to six weeks should give you time to properly plan, prepare, publicize, and produce a successful in-store special event.

## *Evaluating Results*

As you should be able to tell by now, the special event should be working for you on many different levels. It's a way to focus attention. It's a way to entertain, reward, and hold onto your customers. It's a way to teach your target audience more about your product(s) and service(s) so that they will buy more. It's a way to get publicity and build awareness — reaching people with your message even if they never attend your event. It's a way to make your enterprise stand out in a very crowded field.

Each time you hold a special event, you should be asking yourself whether this event is accomplishing all those objectives, as well as any special ones you have earmarked — like introducing a new product. These questions help you evaluate the return on your investment. You should be evaluating each aspect of your special events so you can improve on them next time around.

# Trade and Consumer Shows

Trade and consumer shows can be terrific opportunities for showcasing your product or services — and to obtain business. Like any performer, you need to take the time and attention to produce a blockbuster. The following tips will help you optimize the considerable investment you make when you sign up for exhibit space. Trade and consumer shows afford the PR marketer a time, place, and reason to place strategic messages in the minds of target audiences.

## Help from the Show Management

Take advantage of all the help the show management can offer. The primary advantage of participating in a show is that the show management is responsible for attracting the crowd. If the audience they seek is composed of the customers you seek, everyone will come away happy. If the management is appealing to the general public and you need to reach systems operators, the fit is not a good one.

That said, be aware of how the management plans to promote the show — and see how you can help. The more customers you bring to the show, the better the results overall and the better your relationship will be with the management when you sign up to exhibit again next year. If any aspect of that all-important triangle of customers, exhibitors, and show staff is out of balance, the success of the show is in jeopardy. So help your show management be successful so they can help you be successful.

For example, one consumer show offered all sorts of free collateral for exhibitor distribution to customers. They had copies of the colorful show poster for display in the shop, and color postcards of the same poster art to mail to customers. Exhibitors could paste on simple labels that said "See you at the Show — booth 223!" and send them to all the customers within a three-hour drive of the show location. They even had stickers with the show logo. Order as many of these items as you can — and plan a promotional blitz to let your customers know you'll be attending and where they can find you. Include an incentive to get them to attend and stop by your booth.

Shows that are very promotion-oriented usually make a special effort to attract serious buyers by offering a VIP program. The VIP's pay slightly higher ticket prices to be able to get into the show the day before the general public. In exchange they received a pack of information and special VIP offers — all solicited by the show management from exhibitors. Not only does a "10 percent off" coupon bring people to your booth to see what you have to offer, you can sell more merchandise as a result. Generally, you will stand out as one of only a dozen exhibitors, out of several hundred who take advantage of this showcase opportunity.

Sometimes consumer shows offer to include exhibitor press releases in a special PR mailing they arrange. For less than the cost of sending out 100 releases yourself, you can be a part of a package that goes to all the editors and reporters that should be contacted. Appearing in the company of other high-profile exhibitors, along with the very credible show announcement information gives your business the kind of exposure and validation the editors are looking for.

At any show, the management works very hard at providing entertainment to attendees. Most shows now schedule a whole program of events, from giveaways, to celebrity appearances, to seminars. They need your help to pull these off! For example at every Performance Racing Industry Show (PRI), Chevrolet sells chances to win a small block Chevy engine. The proceeds from the ticket sales went to Muscular Dystrophy research. Every half-hour for the three days of the show an announcement was made over the PA system to remind folks to visit the appropriate booth to buy chances for the engine.

PRI also arranged a program of seminars each day on subjects ranging from cash management to current high-tech Wright-Patterson research projects with potential racing application. The technology session — for the second year in a row — was standing-room only and gave the manufacturer of a hand-held structural flaw sensor that had been piloted an incredible audience. All because the manufacturer had teamed up with PRI to participate. At this show there was another manufacturer with an equally high-tech and high interest subject who went begging for an audience, probably because it wasn't on the advance-billed schedule. The point is — let the show promoters help. If the show you're attending doesn't offer any of these things for exhibitors — suggest they do, and offer to be the first in line!

## *Your Exhibit Space is a Stage*

Consider your exhibit space a stage — and do what it takes to draw an audience.

Trade and consumer shows are theater. If you don't think that's true ask yourself why you're so exhausted after a day of working a booth. It's because you're "on" all day, just as if you were performing on a stage all day. That *is* what you're doing!

Once you see your participation in the show in this way, you'll understand that you need to design a set and costumes to help you present your story, and that you can draw bigger crowds with special effects or a big name star.

Although every show has restrictions on your use of the space you've reserved, especially when it comes to the height of the sides of your display. The basic rule is common courtesy to your neighbor and an attractive presentation for show attendees. If you generate excitement with your display — without causing the exhibitor next door to complain to the show manager — you can do almost anything that's legal.

Different is better. You don't need to spend lots of money on professional trade show displays. That doesn't mean that plastic bags of product hung on peg board is all you need, either. But it does mean that for a manufacturer of storage cases, a display board of polished and machined aluminum is a real dazzler. There are lots of easy-to-set-up display systems out there, but that can be a problem. All the exhibits look the same when they're in the same photos-of-product, catalogs-on-the-counter format. Do something that jars the passersby into looking twice at what you offer. We put a photo of a horse and rider on a display at a consumer boat show. As it happens the waterproof jackets the client was selling worked just as well for equestrians as for sailors, but it really got folks' attention. A PRI exhibitor that does laser cutting of brake rotors and other components had a four-foot tall, three-dimensional dinosaur made of laser-cut aluminum on display.

### Three Tips for Attention-Getting Displays

The three basics for attention-grabbing displays are:

- light and color
- motion
- sound

Unusual signs that are particularly effective include: a large cloth banner for a New Hampshire company that has race results on the Internet. The small (10-foot) booth had a five-foot flag with the company name: goracing.com. Another had the simple three-letter company ID in large plastic letters against a flat background, backlit with a crimson bulb. The third was on a rotor and oscillated at the end of a row of booths, high above the crowd. In an outdoor show, think about balloons. Big ones in unusual shapes.

Sound is also a highly useful draw. Many booths at consumer or trade shows present a video loop of a high-speed action film. This usually draws a crowd, probably because it's such a different medium to look at when your eyes are glazing over after seeing miles of displays. The sound of a video seems to be a great magnet, too. If you have a product that makes an unusual sound, try to figure out a way to offer demonstrations, without driving the management or your fellow exhibitors crazy.

## *Uniforms and Staff Conduct*

Costumes or uniforms are important for exhibitor staff. It would seem obvious in an industry like auto racing that team uniforms play an important role in the overall presentation. Yet a surprising number of PRI exhibitors didn't bother with outfitting the booth staff in uniforms. Aside from the important visual impression of professionalism that uniforms give an exhibitor, they play the extremely critical purpose of telling customers who they can talk to. Customers shouldn't have to go up to someone standing in a booth in a sweater to ask a question, only to be told, "Oh, I don't work here — I'm waiting to talk myself," pointing to another sweater.

If all the staff in your booth have blue sweaters and grey slacks, especially if your company color is blue, your customer will know where to start. The options are endless, from elegant imported sportswear coordinates, to polo shirts with the company logo. Just remember the uniform identifies all of you after hours, as well. Loud exhibitors in the hotel bar are an embarrassment to their employer. Show staff and other exhibitors put the company's general public impression is at stake.

When staff are in the booth they're on stage. Chairs in booths are for customers. This said, it is unrealistic to think that after ten hours on your feet, you're not going to want to sit down. Just do it in a manner that doesn't look like you should be wearing a sign that says "out to lunch." Get up when customers approach. The worst possible set-up for a booth that is supposed to encourage potential customers to strike up conversations with you (so they might buy something) is a counter in the front that separates You from Them. Worse still is the counter, and two chairs in the back where you and your associate are deep in a conversation about where you're going for dinner — or from which you inspect the customers with a bored look on your face. Design the layout to invite people in, not exclude them.

Another thing — most shows now forbid smoking in exhibit areas. You should make the same sort of rule about eating. A cup of coffee or soft drink is one thing; a messy sandwich is another.

Encourage everyone to have a good time. The most successful booths are the ones where the staff and customers are having a good time. Make one of your objectives as an exhibitor to get to know your customers and associates. Also be on the lookout for good ideas other people are using in their booths.

## Premiums

What good are giveaways? It depends. Based on a totally unscientific survey, the Number One "good investment" in trade show paraphernalia is the plastic bag. We all know that people pick up those expensive four color catalogs — and may never look at them again once they lug them home or to their hotel rooms. While they're at the show, they need something to carry all that paper, and imprinted plastic bags are the carrier of choice. The benefit of providing those bags free to customers is that they walk around the show carrying your billboard all day — the modern equivalent of the sandwich board.

Two cautions are in order: 1) It's worth investing in the bigger bag, or your bag will soon go into someone else's bigger sack; and 2) people seem to choose the bags with nicer — or more familiar — graphics. One exhibitor had a dramatic bag with a color photo of a fireworks display replace a variety of other packaging. Another had a simple blue bag with the Goodyear logo and virtually every person who passed the exhibit picked one up.

The other worthwhile premium or giveaway is something extremely visible, and a clever association with your name, product or service. Another key chain or letter opener is a wasted investment. A helium balloon with your logo at a consumer show, that kids can carry around the way their folks carry the plastic bag meets the visibility criterion. The small fluffy penguins that two very attractive models stuck to PRI attendees' shoulders on behalf of the Perma-Cool company were brilliant because they were unusual, cute, and an instant reminder of the company name.

Business card drops or sign-ups to win your product or service are also effective gimmicks — and these give you the information you need for the databases we've talked about in past chapters.

In summary, when it comes to being an exhibitor, just remember, "It's showtime!" Measure everything you plan and do by its intended, and actual, effect on your audience, and you will be well on your way to a successful, productive show.

## *Exhibitor Checklist*

1.  Take advantage of all the help show management offers.

    ❑ Support and participate in show publicity.

    ❑ Participate in VIP programs, contests, and giveaways.

    ❑ Sponsor hospitality.

    ❑ Present a program or seminar.

2.  Make your exhibit space a stage.

    ❑ Design a set and costumes/uniforms to tell your story.

❏ Use special effects or a special guest appearance.

❏ Look out for your show neighbor.

❏ Make sure booth staff understand the conduct you expect of them.

❏ Razzle-dazzle to get passersby to look twice.

❏ Incorporate light, color, and sound.

3. Premiums

❏ Imprinted plastic bags are top choice.

❏ Imprinted helium balloons add visibility.

❏ Choose something clever — a mnemonic — instead of another keychain or pen.

❏ Keep a check on costs; make the premium multi-purpose.

# CHAPTER 10

# Splashing Versus Being Splashed

The difference between a PR person who waits for someone to call and someone who is intelligently and aggressively promoting his or her message is the defining difference of professionalism.

Your job as a PR marketer is to *seek out* opportunities to sell your idea. Your job is to sell, not to take orders. Don't sit around complaining that you don't get any coverage if you're not handing information about business to the people who cover it!

Everything in this book defines what makes an active PR marketing effort. To wrap-up, these are the key issues:

- Timing and advance preparation.
- Professionalism and accuracy
- Understanding your customer and knowing what sells.
- Follow-up.

## Timing and Preparation

Being proactive instead of passive takes attitude, planning, and attitude. As a PR marketer, you are responsible for making sure you know, package, and distribute news about your enterprise before it's old news. Naturally you'll be asked to comment on something that has just happened — usually negative things like a wreck or a takeover or other crisis. Occasionally, someone will surprise you with good news, like an award. In virtually every other category of information you are in a position to provide to the media, you know before they do.

Therefore, you should be able to package the information in a press release, media advisory, or fact sheet and provide it to your media contacts in a timely manner. Timely means both for you and for them. It means understanding their lead times, their typical interview patterns, and their deadlines, as well as your own strategic needs.

For example, if you are announcing a new sponsor, your strategy should be to make the announcement in a way and at a time when you can attract the most media attention: in a press conference at the track on test day, perhaps. If you're announcing a new product, you might time the announcement to be made during a major trade show.

So many companies do this because:

- The media from all over the country who cover the industry are in one place at one time.

- The announcement positions the company as one of the major players in the industry.

- Most of the trade shows go out of their way to showcase new products, and include information about new products and their suppliers in the advance PR they do to attract media and attendees to the show.

Timing is everything in PR. Waiting for the phone to ring just doesn't cut it. To time your announcements and updates perfectly, you obviously need good advance preparation. Basically, you need to develop a reminder system so that the introduction copy for your driver gets sent or faxed to the track announcer the week before you leave. The press kits for the team go in the truck along with all the other racing gear. The recap release on this week's performance and outlook for next week goes out to your media list the day after the race.

The PR marketer maps out the feature opportunities in the trade magazines that relate to your company, knows what the lead times are, and develops a systematic tickler file to make sure the respective reporters are contacted before they finish their stories. They understand that waiting for the reporter to call is not the way to get into the story.

## Professionalism and Accuracy

The proactive PR marketer has to be organized and in command of the information you're presenting. Returning phone calls is critical, as is responding to media inquiries at events out of the office. One of the biggest values of having a regular PR person is that you can delegate the responsibility for answering questions and providing backup information. A PR marketer can also coordinate schedules so that both your and the reporter's needs are met when it comes to interviews.

You have to understand, reporters are attracted to action, that's their job. The more frantically you're working, the more likely a reporter is going to start asking questions. That's why you should develop a Crisis Communications Plan that details who and where your spokesperson will set up headquarters in order to provide responsive answers to the media. No one ever said you have to say everything is great all the time. In fact, you lose credibility — and media interest — if you can be depended upon to give the "no information" answer all the time. But if you proactively understand that they'll be asking, and have a professional approach for accommodating their needs and your own, you will get coverage virtually every time there's a pencil in your vicinity.

## Understand Your Customer and Know What Sells

Your customers are the media; the people who buy your story. The people who are going to act on your information — the consumer of your client's product or service, a sponsor or fans — are second-order customers to the PR marketing effort. Your primary objective has to be attracting media interest and coverage so they can tell your story to a wider audience of consumers than you might otherwise reach. The proactive PR effort, therefore, identifies those customers, just as the best salespeople identify their most likely customers. Both focus on the ones who are their best customers; because in PR marketing as in life, you're much more likely to make repeat sales to the customer you were able to satisfy once. In PR it's called media relations — building rapport with the people who report on your industry.

First of all, you need a current and constantly-evolving list of who your media customers are. Previous chapters have outlined how to keep a database of contacts and why proactive PR people keep a checklist of media names and phone and fax numbers with them at all times. Know what the lead times are, learn what their working habits are. Many sports writers work at night, so it's necessary to fax them information late the day before instead of first thing in the morning. But remember, never fax or e-mail without the recipient's permission. Once you've established the rapport, you won't need to ask every time, but until you do, the only way you can be reasonably sure the reporter will get and read your release is if s/he knows it's coming and knows you only make contact when you have something real to say.

## *Overcoming Objections*

Just as with sales customers, you must overcome objections and satisfy needs in order to earn the sale. Basically, media objections come in two forms: either they don't perceive your story as news; or they feel they've given you too much exposure and want to spread the coverage around. Once you've overcome the objections, it's pretty easy to satisfy a reporter's needs. You answer the questions until they have a story — with the cautionary note that quality and dependability must apply to your information if you expect to sell your product to them again.

Overcoming the objections is a little harder. First, what is news? If you know you have a story because you're better than your competition, you must define better. If you have developed a new product based on leading edge engineering, you must be able to explain both your ideas and the traditional engineering solutions in a way the average, generalist reporter can understand. You'd better be able to at least summarize the difference in a sentence or two before you start drawing pictures on the placemats. Whenever you have the opportunity for a third-party endorsement — an industry award, the purchase of your product by a major customer, even previous publicity — use it to convince reporters that your story is news. When you don't have that leverage, put your news into context. Be creative.

When a reporter tells you, "We just covered you last month," just fill in the reasons you thought s/he might want the most recent news and leave it at that — making sure you continue to send them your regular releases. No reporter ever told a hot item they'd been covered enough. This objection is a good reason for you to review your news packaging and timing to make sure you're delivering what the reporter needs, at the right intervals to stay fresh. Those of you who have Websites should make sure you are constantly updating your information. An Internet surfer who sees the same news and an old date, visit after visit, will react the same way as a reporter who doesn't perceive news in your press releases. They'll go away and you'll have a hard time winning them back.

## Creating Follow-Up

The proactive PR marketer creates reasons for following up with reporters. They listen for clues to their interests, their peeves, their biases. The PR person who is too busy selling his or her own version of information to recognize the human side of the customer will encounter more sales objections than the person who takes the time to turn a byline into a three-dimensional personality.

That's why the people you take on press trips become key allies in future media relations campaigns. You understand how to put your pitch into a context they'll buy.

When you don't yet know a reporter, at least know his or her work. You'll get a much better reception if you call and say, "I saw your article on shock absorbers and have some new information on the subject you might want to keep for next time." More often than not, next time becomes a story focused around your information.

Along the same lines, capitalizing on a trend with a special event or promotion is an excellent means for generating follow-up interest. Run a contest, start a fund-raising campaign, build a fan club. Anything that has a start, middle, and end provides opportunities to announce, update and reward. The point is the continuous communication of real news.

Proactive PR is communication. It's dynamic. It listens as much as it speaks.

## Splashing Requires Focus

Focus on your message. First, you have to know who you are. What is the message you want to get across once you finally have a reporter on the phone or holding a tape recorder to your face? The strongest statement Jeff Gordon makes about Pepsi is when he drinks the stuff at the end of a long, hot race.

The strongest statement — and clearest message — any driver can deliver is that racing is a good thing: it's fun, it's competitive, and everyone involved from sponsor to crew to fan finds it a worthwhile form of entertainment. The more positive associations spokespeople make about racing, the more certain its future, its funding, and its foundations.

For any company, the issue of focus when it comes to your PR message is just as important to futures, funding, and foundation. Too many companies make the mistake of trying to be all things to all people, confusing a misguided attempt to do everything with the idea of reaching every conceivable customer with what you do. For example, you really wonder when Dunkin Donuts decides to branch out into bagels. Or when you see a company that makes a great product let quality slip because they're focused on adding new products, colors, sizes, and dealers to the distribution.

On the other hand, when a Carrera starts putting together a catalog listing the appropriate racing springs and shocks for sports car adaptations, they're not losing focus, they're reaching out to a new market with their focused capability. The message for Carrera is, "we make performance suspension components."

## Focus on Your Audience

Focusing your message brings coherence to your marketing effort. Once you decide what you want your audiences to know when they hear your name or see your logo, it's much easier to figure out where to put that logo when it comes to advertising, sponsorship, and PR. It's a common mistake to waste time and money on getting your name in the paper, when in fact, it would be more profitable to get your name in front of people who will actually buy from you.

Pick your audience, your media, and your message so they all line up logically, and the elements will work together to get you more bang for the buck.

Focus tends to help you avoid the over-extension problems that plague businesses, especially start-ups. It's also an often-heard rationale for the "but we've never done that before" attitude, which brings us to the next important point.

## Focus on a Point Down the Road

If you're focused on today, you're heading for a collision just the same as if you were concentrating on the back bumper of the car ahead of you.

If all you do is chase the competition, you could follow them right off the road. If you have a focus on where you want to be a year, or five years from now, you're much more likely to accomplish your objective. If every article and every special event your company participates in conveys the same future goals, your potential customers and sponsors will have a clearer picture of what they can get from you. Putting your future plans into print also has the added benefit of helping you commit to them.

## The Importance of Follow-Through

The most inspired publicity and business plans can fail if there's no commitment to getting the job done. By focusing on the message you want to communicate and on choosing the right media for the message, you create an action plan that helps you actually place the stories you'd love to see reporters write about you.

The mark of an amateur PR plan is the placement generalization. If your PR expert is saying, "We will contact the trade magazines" instead of "*Lodging Hospitality* is planning an article on renovations in April. Let's call Ed Watkins and see who's doing the story so we can talk about the $40 million we just spent," that person is not focused on the goals.

When you have a specific plan of known editorial opportunities, and known company events such as product introductions and new target markets, you have a focused action plan that has a greater chance of being done.

Your plan should be a working template, not a vague outline, and you should be following through on all the great ideas you came up with when the plan was developed, or you might as well not have wasted the time spent creating it. The more specific — the more focused — the plan, the better you can estimate and track your results.

## The Plan and the PR Template

Without a formal, written PR plan, you will forget to prepare the obvious and you will miss the easy opportunities for getting your client's name out there. By preparing a plan and a timing template, detailing what you want to accomplish, you will avoid the last-minute panic that sets in when you realize you've missed a deadline or you're not sufficiently prepared for an event.

## Step by Step

To build your plan and template, write down the events you want to publicize on a calendar grid, and work backwards. Plot the months between now and your event across the top of your form and fill in the key events. For a hotel opening you might have groundbreaking, topping-off, mass-hiring, hard-hat tour, soft opening, and grand opening. Fill in the approximate dates for the following:

- Interview key people
- Draft press release
- Create invitation list
- Create media list
- Outline catering requirements
- Distribute press release and invitations
- Follow-up
- Fax media advisories
- Hire photographer
- Write speeches
- Order special decorations
- Event
- Release, photo, caption distribution

You'll also want to include several rows for media relations, organized by type of media. In these rows, detail story opportunities listed in the publications' editorial calendars. You can prepare a separate publicity template that lists all the media you've contacted, by name and date.

Your template should also include opportunities to support each major event. For example, by-lines prepared by members of the development team that you want to place in the local business journal or details of a charity event you're sponsoring in the new hotel. As you work the plan, you can make notes on the outcomes, cross-reference your clip analysis, and add in opportunities that arise as you move toward the event. The template becomes a working document in front of you every day, getting dog-eared and covered with notes. You won't forget anything critical and your client will perceive it — and you — as a professional effort.

After the event, prepare an informal audit of your effort to determine what worked and what didn't, what you need to change, things you wish you had known before you started. This audit will provide benchmarks against which you can measure what you achieve next year.

## A Quick Summary

When you define your identity, you make it easier to explain who you are to the people you want publicity from. Set goals, establish focus, and position your identity, in a line or two you can explain to people who don't have your expertise, but perceive that your field is a hot news subject. The less muddled your definitions, the more success you'll have in getting your message across.

A PR marketing professional must organize the tools:

1. Define your audiences.
2. Create a database of names and addresses for your audiences.
3. Identify media lead times and create a press release schedule.
4. Create collateral.
5. Reinforce the identity and positioning of your client.
6. Create incentives for fans and product or service customers.
7. Leverage event promotion.
8. Recap, benchmark, and plan.

As PR marketer you maintain the image and awareness of your company, client, group, or sponsor. Their professionalism is, inevitably, judged by the professionalism of your communications effort. Be clear, accurate, honest, and organized and you will reap the rewards in publicity, attendance, and sponsorship. Splash — or be splashed.

# Sample Hotel Public Relations Standards Manual

## *I. The Role of Public Relations*

### 1. Definition

Public relations is more than just publicity, special events or community programs; it is the ongoing process of building relationships and trust with the various people or audiences who influence a company's success. In the hotel industry, these audiences include guests, employees, business and community leaders, travel professionals, investors, and industry partners.

The role of public relations at X Hotel Company is to interpret the actions of the corporation and its properties, through a strategic communications program in order to favorably impress its audiences. From the development of a world-class resort to the launch of a new marketing program, the public relations opportunity for every activity should be planned in advance to maximize its effects on public opinion and financial goals.

Your hotel is a critical link in our global communications process. In this Public Relations Standards Manual, we will discuss the role of public relations at the corporate and property level and outline specific policies and practices to promote consistent and efficient PR communication throughout the organization. The prevailing objective is to create a powerful, consistent worldwide image that keeps your hotel positively positioned in the public eye and one step ahead of the competition.

## 2. Property Public Relations

While public relations at the corporate or chain level is focused on the big picture of the company at large, local hotels must tailor public relations activities to their own audiences based on individual projects, goals, and messages. Each X Hotel has its own marketing goals and, as a result, a unique set of publics with that to communicate. The role of property-level public relations is to create positive communications programs that support the individual hotel while promoting the X Hotels brand name.

At the local level, creative public relations can give an added boost to an already well-run hotel. Public relations can provide a cost-efficient and powerful support or alternative to advertising. Equally important, property public relations can:

- help improve employee relations;
- position the hotel as a community leader; and
- build successful liaisons with other influential local audiences such as customers, local media, and the community.

## II. Aligning Public Relations with the Sales and Marketing Plan

### 1. Matching Public Relations with Sales Objectives

Public Relations is frequently misunderstood to be "getting the hotel (or general manager's) name in the paper." While publicity campaigns are certainly contributory tools to achieving the overall objectives of telling the company's story to its key audiences and inducing favorable opinions and actions from these audiences, publicity is the outcome, not the practice of public relations.

The best public relations programs support sales objectives; and the best PR plans are written in concert with the sales and marketing plan. By echoing the goals of the sales and marketing plan the public relations activities have clear direction and reinforce the sales and marketing tactics that are being used to generate the intended results.

Public relations tools and tactics that can be brought to bear on the achievement of sales and marketing objectives include:

- Sales promotions (that usually involve a short-term price or product);
- Special events tailored to showcase a new service, facility or hotel benefit;

- Newsletters that provide a fuller picture of a capability (such as food and beverage), product (such as a loyalty program), or individual property;

- Sponsorships, that reinforce the image of X Hotels or an individual X Hotel;

- Partnership marketing programs that cross-promote two complementary businesses; and

- Media relations efforts that build long-term relationships with key editors and writers (through press trips, background sessions, professional networking, and the like) that will bear fruit at a future, often highly useful, moment.

## 2. Strategic Targeting of Market Segments

Public relations, especially the media relations and promotional effort, should logically follow the sales plan, prioritizing messages, and target audiences in tandem with the sales objectives.

For example, if the focus for the next quarter is on maximizing rate, the public relations effort should focus on short-term media efforts to reach the highest-spending market segment: the transient corporate traveler. If the focus is on building occupancy to fill need periods, the public relations program should detail promotional programs to attract guests and target those media who cover promotional opportunities. If the objective for the year is to maximize occupancy and rate, the target would be a broad spectrum of media with messages tailored to elicit response from decision makers in each market segment.

## 3. Including Public Relations in the Marketing Plan

By understanding the breadth of communications assistance that effective public relations can offer a marketing effort, all of us who are responsible for ensuring the success of X Hotels gain an important, strategic advantage against the competition. Because the tools of successful public relations generate opinions and attitudes, the PR program that has been integrated in the sales and marketing plan actually influences decision makers in measurable ways.

The Marketing Plan which includes strategic and tactical public relations details benefits from opportunities no other marketing discipline can offer — free exposure and third-party credibility.

## III. *Public Relations Department Functions*

### 1. Individual Properties

The responsibilities of this department are:

- Maintain the communications profile of the hotel, its products and services, and its executives (see Section V).
- Serve as liaison with the X Public Relations Department to effect communications programs and to raise awareness of opportunities for strategic and tactical marketing communications.
- Manage all media relations efforts that pertain specifically to the property, disseminating information in a timely, proactive manner, and responding to all local inquiries.
- Provide a professional link between local media and the corporate Public Relations departments, both for referring inquiries of a company-wide nature and for reinforcing (and creating) relationships with strategic writers and editors who are nationally-oriented and locally-based.
- Execute national promotions locally and creating/implementing promotions for the individual hotel.
- Create and executes communications and promotional programs that effectively maximize local market segment databases.
- Serve as liaison with local and regional community organizations on behalf of the hotel.
- Support employee relations and communications initiatives.

## IV.  *Policies and Procedures*

### 1. Chain Communications Messages

The Chain Public Relations Department manages, and in some cases, fills, the spokesperson role for the company. All communications with the media (print and electronic), with owners/investors, employees, and the customer publics should be channeled through the Public Relations Department to ensure consistency and continuity of messages, accuracy, and follow-up to ensure that any subsequent questions are answered.

It is important to note that there are certain matters only designated spokespersons should discuss with the press. As a general rule, Public Relations department members should not speak to the press on sensitive subjects such as financial and business matters, crises or political issues.

Statements will have more credibility coming from a senior officer of the company who is in a position to conjecture and make company commitments that cannot be made by a PR director.

The Public Relations Department will confirm and issue the following announcements in the form of press releases and electronic messages following their approval by the President of the company.

### a. Hotel Portfolio and Additions
Announcements in this category include:

- newly-built hotels
- purchased hotels

Announcements should occur when an acquisition or groundbreaking date is determined, when senior staff are selected, at the soft opening and at the grand opening.

Head-office Public Relations is also responsible for providing current information to those trade publications that publish annual portfolio surveys.

A senior executive(s) should be positioned as the spokesperson(s) regarding the company's growth plans, and made available for interviews, speaking opportunities and other proactive communications roles.

### b. Appointments and HR Programs
Chain-level Public Relations is usually responsible for announcing all appointments and promotions from the level of General Manager and higher.

In the case of the most senior executive staff, the most senior Public Relations Office is responsible for issuing announcements to the daily print and electronic business press.

These announcements should include:

- correct title and a brief description of responsibilities;
- brief statement of whom the new person is replacing, and in the case of a promotion, why;
- previous experience relevant to the position;
- a statement from the hiring executive on the candidate's capabilities; and
- a formal portrait photograph of the executive.

Chain-level Public Relations is also responsible for announcements covering any HR program or policy that affects the entire company. This office should also pursue media and speaking opportunities for the senior executives of the company to be positioned as experts in their respective areas of responsibility.

### c. Financial Disclosure

Chain-level Public Relations is responsible for issuing statements on the financial success and accomplishments of the company. These statements must come from the highest level because of their impact on the international identity of the company and because of the role they play in communicating the expansion and development of the company to current and potential investors.

This office is responsible for issuing any and all required financial disclosures stemming from its operating licenses or other jurisdictional privileges, such as reporting to investors, and senior executives participating in financial incentive programs.

The Chief Financial Officer and other designated senior officers of the company, should be positioned as spokespersons for financial matters and made available for interviews, speaking opportunities, and other proactive communications roles.

## 2. Property Communication Messages

### a. Facilities, Services and Amenities

The Property PR Department is responsible for announcements of any new facilities, services, and amenities to the appropriate media targeting key hotel market segments.

### b. Appointments and HR Programs

The Property PR Department is responsible for:

- Maintaining current biographies for each of the members of the hotel's Executive Team;
- Distributing appointment announcements to local, regional, "hometown," alumni and professional association publications;
- Assisting with local distribution of Appointments and Global HR program announcements;
- Publicizing HR initiatives that position the hotel as a rewarding place to work;

- Publicizing HR initiatives that position the hotel as a "good neighbor;" and
- Positioning the hotel's HR executive as an expert in the local HR and business community.

### c. Sales and Marketing Programs

The Property PR Department is responsible for:

- Maintaining current press releases on each individual marketing program operated by the hotel;
- Assisting with local distribution of X Hotels Sales and Marketing program announcements and collateral;
- Securing local publicity about property sales and marketing initiatives that help position the hotel to customers and potential customers in keeping with the Marketing Plan;
- Assisting the property sales and marketing team with creating and implementing initiatives/events that draw positive attention to the hotel and its capabilities and services; and
- Securing local publicity about one-time property sales and marketing initiatives/events that are unusual and newsworthy.

### d. Systems and Operations Programs

The Property PR Department is responsible for:

- Maintaining current press releases on each key system and operations program operated by the hotel;
- Assisting with local distribution of X Hotels Systems and Operations program announcements and collateral;
- Securing local publicity about property systems and operations initiatives that help position the hotel to customers and potential customers; and
- Securing local publicity about property systems and operations programs and personnel that are unusual and newsworthy.

### e. Corporate Programs

The Property Public Relations Department is responsible for relaying information to X Hotels Communications staff for newsletters and other purposes, and providing news of national and international interest to X Hotels Public Relations Department for additional exposure and coordination with news from other properties.

## V. *Public Relations Department Operations*

## 1. Materials

### a. Press Kit

The purpose of a press kit is to provide all the basic information a reporter or editor needs. The most effective press kits present this information in a quickly-referenced form. A press kit should be prepared with the understanding that no one will ever read it cover-to-cover; so key points should be reiterated and cross-referenced.

The property press kit should include:

- Corporate Fact Sheet and Backgrounder
- Property Fact Sheet that details address, phone, fax, e-mail, executive team, total number of rooms, number, and dimensions of meeting spaces, description of restaurant(s), brief descriptions of property Sales and Marketing and Systems and Operations programs, and special facilities
- Property History
- Property Backgrounder
- Biographies of Key Executives, including:
  - General Manager
  - Director of Sales and Marketing
  - Executive Chief
- Press releases on key marketing programs
- Press releases on Services and Amenities such as:
  - Meeting capabilities
  - Restaurant specialties, programs and promotions
  - On-site health and fitness capabilities
  - Corporate traveler business services and benefits
- Directory
- Property Brochure(s)
- Reprints of Articles — professionally printed copies of favorable profiles of the hotel, personnel, and marketing initiatives that position the hotel relative to its competitive niche.
- Business Card — For the Public Relations Director and general manager.

## b. Photography

The Public Relations Department should maintain a current file of photographs and sufficient duplicates to allow the Department to meet Sales and Marketing and media requests for photography.

The photo library should include:

- Color and black and white property photos of the following:
  - exterior
  - interior — lobby
  - interior — restaurant(s)
  - interior — guestrooms (each configuration)
  - interior — front desk
  - interior — distinctive artwork or architectural feature
  - interior — fitness center, business center and other facilities
  - interior — meeting rooms
- Color and black and white management photos
- Formal portraits of senior executives, including:
  - General Manager
  - Director of Sales and Marketing
  - Executive Chef
- Product and Event Photos: Illustrations of key sales and marketing and systems and operations features or initiatives:
  - front office/reservations center
  - menu feature
  - special events

## c. Media Resources

The property Public Relations Department should maintain the following tools and resources in current, accurate, easily-referenced condition:

- National Consumer Media Lists: A list of North American travel editors and travel writers who regularly report on travel and the cities where X Hotels properties are located, with special emphasis on writers within the hotel's city and region.
- Local and regional media lists including magazine, newspaper, professional newsletters and electronic outlets.
- Trade Media Lists: A list of editors and reporters who regularly report on the hotel industry and the travel trade (travel agents, meetings, and corporate travel).

- Editorial Calendars: Current editorial calendars for trade and such consumer media should be annotated to highlight opportunities for placements, noting the lead-times required for media contact.

## 4. Tracking and Analysis

### a. Clipping Service

It is helpful when trying to track the impact of a Public Relations effort to be able to review all of the media placements that occur as a result of the distribution of press releases, calls and letters to editors, and the like. The best way to manage the collection of PR clips is to hire a Clipping Service.

Burrelle's, and others, maintain subscriptions to all of the magazines and newspapers likely to carry news about the hotels. Once the clipping service is hired, the service's readers scan all of the publications, clip and collect stories that answer the description supplied (e.g., all mentions of the Hotel, the restaurant, the following executives). The clips are then tallied and forwarded to the Public Relations Department on a monthly basis.

### b. Clipping Analysis

In addition to merely reading and clipping articles about a particular Hotel, the clipping service will, for an additional fee, provide analysis. A report accompanying the clips could include:

- types of publication (newspaper, magazine)
- state-by-state breakdown
- readership of the publications
- coverage of a press release
- dollar value of placements based on advertising rates

### c. Promotions Tracking

While a clipping service will provide information about where a particular story or press release appeared, this information will not detail the response a promotion or program generated. To track response, there needs to be a direct link between the promotion and the guest or restaurant customer.

Some of the most effective "links" include:

- Distinctive names for room types or packages so that the Reservations Department and Sales and Marketing can keep track of inquiries and bookings that come over the telephone.

- Special telephone number used only for the particular promotion.
- Coupons, ads, postcards, or tickets that are redeemed to give the guest or client access to the program or promotion. These printed vehicles should capture the customer's name, address, and an indication of other programs that may be of interest.
- Website "hits" and other interactive data collection opportunities.

It is important to build in a tracking system because the results of a promotion are only as good as the data collected. If tracking is not constant and consistent, the findings are inconclusive and will not give an indication of whether the effort has been economically effective or worth repeating.

# Sample Hotel Crisis Communications Plan

To be successful in controlling the potential damage the company or individual hotel might incur in the case of a crisis, those responsible for maintaining the professional communications must be prepared to respond. In order not to be caught off-guard, and to reduce the inherent risk, the Corporate PR Department, Corporate Marketing Department, and each Hotel maintains a current, practical Crisis Communications Plan.

While the Plan should enable an individual property to respond instantly to any crisis, direct communication with the senior-most office should be maintained throughout the emergency.

## 1. The Crisis Communications Plan should include:

- Definitions of what constitutes a crisis such as fire, accidents, death or illness, storms, acts of terrorism, strike, financial uncertainty, or violations of law or local custom that would adversely affect the marketability of the hotel or its parent company.

- Specification of the crisis spokesperson and his or her responsibilities and authority to the exclusion of all others unless designated; plus the names of two backup spokespersons.

- Emergency contact phone numbers, including home and cell phone numbers for the senior staff
- Designation of where the Crisis Command will be established, both within the building and off-site in the event the building is unusable
- Designation of a Media Center, separate from the Command Center, where telephones, electrical hook-ups (generators in the case of electrical failure), and refreshments will be made available
- Basic scripts for the spokesperson and scripts and relaying instructions for the telephone operator in the initial response to the crisis
- Plan of action for evacuation of and communication with corporate staff in the event of an emergency in the headquarters offices
- Timetable for media and staff communications updates by the spokesperson
- List of authorities who would be spokespersons in the course of any investigation or ongoing situation, such as fire or police action
- Basic scripts and checklist of follow-up actions necessary for wrap-up
- Procedures for internal communications

## *2. Naming a Spokesperson*

### The Role of the Spokesperson

The Spokesperson in a crisis has two main media responsibilities:

- Providing timely, accurate information to the media in the most proactive manner possible.
- Maintaining the reputation of the hotel or company as a caring, responsible, law-abiding citizen and business.

At times, these objectives can seem to conflict. This is why the crisis spokesperson must be a person of authority who commands respect, fosters credibility, and can remain calm and in control in emergency situations. In most cases, the General Manager has the training, experience, and background to handle such responsibility. The two backup spokespersons should be trained and briefed to be able to perform this critical role in the event the General Manager is not available to fulfill the function.

### The Role of the Public Relations Director

Someone other than the Public Relations Director should be the spokesperson in a crisis. It is imperative that the Public Relations Director (with his or her knowledge of the media and relationships with media representatives likely to be assigned to cover the story) can assist the Crisis Spokesperson by serving as liaison between the spokesperson and the media.

The Public Relations Director should not interpret or elaborate on the statements of the spokesperson. The Public Relations Director should:

- Direct the operations of the Media Center.
- Disseminate the statements made by the spokesperson to the media.
- Identify potential media allies and adversaries.
- Be proactive in providing follow-up for media, when indicated.
- Act as liaison between the spokesperson and any public officials concerned.
- Ensure that commentary is restricted to the spokesperson and that staff persons are not available to the media for comment.
- Ensure that staff (and their families') needs are addressed.

## 3. Dealing with the Media

After notifying the spokesperson and activating the command center, the next step is to activate the Media Center. The professional impression of the company's ability to respond to and control a crisis situation is made at the very start of a crisis. If the crisis is severe enough, a Media Center, equipped with the necessary tools for reporters, should be established.

In any event, the spokesperson must make him or herself available to the media at the earliest opportunity, once the basic facts have been determined. Right from the start, the spokesperson should establish that regular briefings will be provided. After identifying the authorized spokesperson backup, the spokesperson should reinforce that any comments coming from anyone other than the designated or public officials involved, such as fire or police chief, are speculative and may even impair the resolution of the crisis.

Those who have experienced crisis communications first-hand report that success depends on responsiveness, candor, and the understanding of what the media are trying to accomplish in their coverage of the story.

## 4. Post-Crisis Management

The actions of the hotel towards its guests, clients, employees, and other audiences following the resolution of a crisis are as important to the maintenance of goodwill, identity, and market positioning as any initiative undertaken in less-stressful times. Because these audiences are expecting the hotel to be wrapped up in its internal examination of what caused the crisis, any outreach effort generously extended by the hotel will come as a pleasant surprise that exceeds the audiences' expectations.

As soon as is practicably possible, the hotel should communicate with every audience that was involved or impacted by the crisis, reinforcing the hotel's ability to cope with the situation, its staff's preparation for controlling crises, the fact that the hotel has returned to "business as usual"; or, if necessary, detailing whatever pre-determined plans have been put in place to work around any impediments caused by the crisis until everything is back to normal.

The role of the Public Relations Director following the resolution of the crisis includes:

- Drafting the appropriate thank-you letters to public officials for the General Manager.
- Providing a wrap-up statement, where appropriate, to media contacts with the goal of preserving the image and positioning that has been cultivated with those contacts.
- Leading the team that addresses the appropriate response to employees and guests.
- Leading the post-crisis critique of the Crisis Communications Plan.

# Sample
# PR Plan

This appendix offers an example of the strategic thinking that should guide any total PR effort. Although it is specific to motorsports, the "best practices" are the same. Simply substitute your own industry and its key audiences and benchmarks and you'll have a summary of everything detailed in previous chapters and a useful start for building a working PR plan.

These basics cover roughly eight categories; but the first thing you and your client must decide is "who are you?" You should define, in a line or two, your format, coverage, and key associations.

Winston Cup is the premier North American Stock Car (NASCAR) series. The Indy Racing League (IRL) started out as the American open wheel defender of the Indy 500 tradition. International Super-Modified Association (ISMA), on the other hand, frequently runs into problems positioning itself beyond its acronym. Some of the teams want ISMA to be the premier professional series for supermodifieds; while others want to retain the original club feel to the series.

When you define your purpose, you make it easier to explain who you are to editors, potential customers, sponsors, and fans, and to the untapped resources who don't currently follow your industry but perceive that it's a hot property. The more muddled the definitions, the more confused these rookies are. And the more likely they are to maintain such stereotypes as, "stock car racing is just a regional Southern thing."

In the chapter on Press Releases, the suggestion was made to add a positioning line to all your press releases, along the lines of, "Based in Newfields, New Hampshire, Leading Edge Motorsport provides set-up engineering and motorsports marketing services to street and race performance clientele."

A racing series positioning line might be, "Winston Pro-Stock at Lee USA Speedway makes the excitement of professional NASCAR competition accessible and affordable to local teams, fans, and businesses."

Once you have positioned your series, you can outline the PR basics for promoting the circuit.

## Define Your Audiences

Audiences are those categories into which you can divide the people you want to attract as customers. For a race series, your audiences include:

- Drivers, teams, and owners
- Tracks
- Sponsors, including the title sponsor
- Fans
- Media

## Create a Database of Names and Addresses for Your Audiences

Every entry on your lists should include a person's name — not just "Promoter," "Owner," or "Editor." The surest route to the rotary file is the PR equivalent of the occupant label. If you can't take the time to address your information to the appropriate specific person, what makes you think he or she has the time to listen to what you're saying? Lists that are kept current, are your single most valuable resource as a PR professional.

Basic PC programs allow you to set up fairly sophisticated databases of names, addresses, and phone/fax/e-mail data. With the information databased rather than simply typed-up on lists, you can create professional mailings quickly and easily, personally addressing letters, printing envelopes instead of using labels, and so on. You can also annotate your files right in the computer — so you can keep track of reporters' deadlines, for example, or simple tracking for fan loyalty programs, and the like. Your track list should include the owner and the promoter/PR person.

Your sponsor list should include both local and national sponsors — you know, all those brands listed on the side of the Officials' truck? Again, get the specific names and addresses of the person you need to keep current on what's happening in the series they sponsor. In an ideal world, the series teams would understand that you're doing them a service to keep their sponsors updated on news for their circuit; but in the real world, you're unlikely to be able to pry those contacts from the teams. Having those contacts will allow you to generate wider publicity for the sponsor and the series, will help you boost awareness for motorsports in the general business community, and will produce more warm fuzzies than sponsor raids. The role of the professional PR person requires a considerable amount of professionalism, honesty, and discretion. If your series doesn't respect you — and you don't respect their confidentiality — none of you will get far.

When it comes to your media database, remember to include:

- Reporters assigned by the local/regional racing papers to cover your series.
- Sports reporters assigned to the series by the local daily and weekly newspapers, TV, and radio.
- Business editors of the local weeklies, dailies, and business media.
- Sports reporters for your local weeklies, dailies, TV, and radio who don't assign someone to motorsports.
- Editors of trade magazines whose industries are represented by your series and teams' sponsors.
- Editors of national racing publications — print and electronic — who cover your series. Don't forget NASCAR On-line if you're handling a NASCAR touring series, or goracing.com for news about several dozen series.

## *Identify Media Lead Times and Create a Press Release Schedule*

There's nothing older than last week's racing results when your cars are lined up on the track for this week's start. The same is true for any news — when everyone else knows it already, you can't sell it to a reporter. As a series PR person, for example, you have to be the official provider of results to all interested parties, as soon as those results are declared official. In this age of electronic communication, you can have your race press release on-line within an hour of the finish. Set up the systems that allow you to accomplish that goal:

- Find out how and when the reporters want your results and high-lights — what are their lead times and when are they at their desks?

- Enter their e-mail addresses in your address book, and their fax numbers in your broadcast fax system — assuming you have these capabilities. Or keep the phone numbers for call-in sports results with you so you can call from the track.

- Copy checklists of names so you can quickly run down the list of those you've been able to reach, who needs follow-up, whose fax was busy.

You have multiple opportunities to publicize your series, the individual races, and the drivers and teams. By creating a press release schedule in advance, you can save yourself the anxiety of forgetting to promote a major event or component of the series (like the Rookie of the Year standings) until it's too late. At minimum, you should send out the following releases:

- The results and highlights of every race.

- An advance on the next race: date, track, time, number of entries, plus any special contests, gate prizes, "kids free" offers or other promotions the track has arranged.

- Weekly rookie of the year update. This release should include a pre-approved "blurb" from the sponsor to reinforce their association with the award, preferably a different one in each release.

- A monthly, or more frequent, update on the series — highlights, human interest notes.

- Monthly releases on season-long promotions you have coordinated with your tracks and sponsors.

In addition, you can generate publicity by focusing on the personal stories in each team — ask your teams what their hometown papers are, and talk to those editors about the excitement of racing as it's happening in their own backyard.

You can generate trade coverage for motorsports (thereby attracting interest from more potential sponsors in that industry) by suggesting a story on why XYZ Manufacturing is sponsoring a stock car on your circuit to the *Manufacturer's Monthly* editor.

You could pitch the local business editor on the impact of your series' race-track(s) on the local economy: the money invested by the teams, sponsors, track, and concession.

The possibilities are endless.

## *Create Series Collateral*

Collateral is the generic name for all those brochures, flyers, and folders that contain marketing information. In the case of a race series, the two key pieces of collateral are the schedule and the press kit.

The basic race series schedule is a laminated or glossy-stock pocket card, that lists the dates, locations, and times for every race in your series. The cover has your title sponsor's logo. Other series sponsor logos should appear somewhere on the card, too. Print enough for the total attendance of all of your races — that should give you enough to give each of your teams sufficient quantities to hand out to their sponsors' businesses, their fans clubs, etc. Make it a value-added piece and you'll be able to find support financing to print huge quantities. For example, if you include the logos and/or phone numbers of all of the tracks, they might fund a single schedule card. Or you might find a regional sponsor who wants to get his feet wet in motorsports sponsorship to pay for the card.

The press kit should be an encyclopedic source of information on your series for the media and for the teams trying to attract sponsors to the series. Therefore, the press kit should contain:

- Fact sheet containing the names, address, and phone numbers of key contacts, the number of cars competing, the geographic scope of the teams/series, total audiences, key media coverage (for example, if all races are carried by a local TV station), the specs for the cars.

- Backgrounder on the series — history, positioning statement.
- The race schedule, including tracks and dates.
- Track demographics.
- List of teams — driver names, car make/model and number, team owner.
- List of sponsors — race, tracks, and teams.
- Series highlights — graduates who have gone on to higher racing levels, personalities, officials.
- For series that are divisions of national sanctioning bodies — like NASCAR or NHRA — there should be a backgrounder on that organization, as well.

Another useful piece of collateral is the newsletter. A monthly newsletter gives you the platform to reiterate the progress of the series (overall points as well as the rookie race) and the involvement of your series sponsors. You can also promote upcoming races and venues, track the progress of season-long incentives, profile emerging stars, behind the scene heroes and other human-interest stories, and capture the highlights.

The newsletter should be mailed to everyone in your database.

## *Promote Your Sponsor*

As series PR director, you are responsible for reinforcing the identity and positioning of your series sponsor. At minimum this means including their logo on your press release letterhead, press kits, and race schedules. It also means that you should be in contact with that sponsor's regional or national motorsports marketing director so that s/he can funnel shell press releases, product announcements, and promotional ideas to you. Having a series sponsor contact also means that you can get sponsor endorsements and quotes for your press releases from senior executives within the sponsoring company, adding professionalism and credibility to your messages.

Beyond those basics, look for opportunities to publicize what your sponsor does for your series. As we all know, the loyalty fans have for motorsports sponsors and their products is phenomenal. Remind your fans that Busch, Coca Cola or Craftsman is the reason their favorite driver is able to compete, so that they can repay that sponsor by buying their products. Remember to keep that sponsor informed, so they can track the results and give you credit for them!

## Create Incentives for Fans Who Follow the Whole Series

Drivers are rewarded by the point standings; but what about the fans who turn out, week after week, to eat your track(s)' hot dogs and cheer on their favorites? Smart track promoters have made it easy for fans to make motorsports a family activity, with autograph sessions, kids' nights, parades, and parachutes. How hard is it to reward the faithful with a tangible "thank you"?

Loyalty programs were invented by the airlines to give passengers a reason to pick one indistinguishable airline seat over another. Even before that, doughnut shops were encouraging volume purchases by offering a baker's dozen to customers they wanted to make "regulars."

These incentives accomplish two important objectives:

- They reward people for a particular behavior and give them a reason to come back for more.
- They're an opportunity to publicize what you're doing.

If your reward for attending every race in a series is a visible badge, like a pin or hat, they have the added benefits of:

- Making the recipient feel special — as if you've moved the barricades for them.
- Attracting attention from "outsiders" who want to know what the pin or hat signifies.

Everyone in motorsports marketing bears responsibility for promoting awareness of the sport. Familiar marketing tools like human interest stories and incentive programs help us showcase what we're doing for mainstream audiences (and reporters) who are otherwise embarrassed by the fact that they can't tell the difference between CART and a Go Kart.

## Leverage Track Promotion

In many cases a series PR director is also the track promoter for the series' venue. But for touring series, the PR director must work in unison with the track promoters to get the most bang for everybody's buck.

Early before the start of every season you should identify yourself to all your tracks' promoters — preferably in person. Give them a copy of your press kit, talk about their plans for your race date, and discuss how you can help develop promotions with that race's sponsor, with the track's sponsors, supporters, and media. Together you can leverage the track promotion and your series' efforts (like the loyalty program we discussed above) to produce a win-win situation for both of you: more fans, more entries, and more press coverage.

## Recap, Benchmark, and Plan

At the end of the season, your job is to prepare the annual report to your series' shareholder — the teams and owners, the sponsors, and the fans. Your annual report, like your monthly newsletter is your opportunity to showcase the results your efforts have produced. It's an invaluable summary for use by the media, in seeking sponsors for next year (for the series, the tracks, and the teams) and it lets your sanctioning body know what you've accomplished, too.

In addition to the formal report, you should prepare an informal audit for yourself of what worked and what didn't, what you need to change, and things you wish you had known before you started. This audit will provide benchmarks against which you can measure what you achieve next year.

As PR director you maintain the image and awareness of your series. The professionalism of the circuit is, inevitably, judged by the professionalism of your communications effort. Be clear, accurate, honest, and organized and your series will reap the rewards in publicity, attendance, and sponsorship.

# *Index*

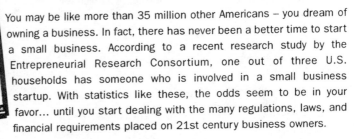

# From The Leading Publisher of Small Business Information
# Books that save you time and money.

Focuses not on prescribing the "best" marketing method, but on using a combination of dozens of marketing techniques, employed by advertising professionals. Teaches the reader how to evaluate many marketing angles, and become better prepared for the challenges of marketing in the new century.

**Marketing for the New Millennium**                    **Pages: 200**
**Paperback: $19.95          ISBN: 1-55571-432-3**

Written by a small business attorney with extensive experience representing consultants. Explains everything a consultant needs to know about the law to properly structure and operate a consulting business. Judy Gedge presents the material in a practical and concrete fashion that answers questions commonly posed by consultants. Also contains a sample consulting agreement, subcontractor's agreement, and a resource directory.

**A Legal Road Map for Consultants**                    **Pages: 125**
**Paperback: $18.95          ISBN: 1-55571-460-9**

This sales training guide is specifically for those selling expensive items and interacting face-to-face with consumers. It explains how to employ a winning approach even when stakes are high, and gives insights into patterns of buying exclusive products, so that the seller has a greater sense of comfort through the sales process and exercises more control over its outcome. Author Hal Slater speaks from experience as a three-time recipient of General Motors' highest sales award.

**Secrets to High-Ticket Selling**                    **Pages: 200**
**Paperback: $19.95          ISBN: 1-55571-422-6**

Using dozens of real-life examples author Gerald Baron shows how building a relationship is the key to business development and personal fulfillment. By using the book's common-sense principles you can develop strategic relationships that take the concept of "relationship marketing" one step further.

**Friendship Marketing**                    **Pages: 230**
**Paperback: $18.95          ISBN: 1-55571-399-8**

ALL MAJOR CREDIT CARDS ACCEPTED

CALL TO PLACE AN ORDER
— or —
TO RECEIVE A FREE CATALOG
# 1-800-228-2275

International Orders (541) 479-9464          Fax Orders (541) 476-1479
Web site http://www.psi-research.com          Email sales@psi-research.com

PSI Research   P.O. Box 3727   Central Point, Oregon   97502   U.S.A.

# From The Leading Publisher of Small Business Information
# Books that save you time and money.

Pursuing a high-tech business has never been more opportune, however the competition in the industry is downright grueling. Author Richard Manweller brings a smart, in-depth strategy with motivational meaning. It will show you how to tailor your strategy to grain investor's attention. If you are looking for a financial angel, Funding High-Tech Ventures is the guidance you need to make the right match.

**Funding High-Tech Ventures**                                      **Pages: 160**
**Paperback: $21.95**          **ISBN: 1-55571-405-6**

Learn how to position your products correctly in the international marketplace and how to begin the process of exploring sales avenues outside of the United States. Stresses the practical key differences of selling to foreign markets; how to find the all-important local marketing agents; covers required product and label changes; and gives advice on handling requests for under-the-table payoffs. Real-life example are highlighted throughout.

**Developing International Markets**                                 **Pages: 350**
**Paperback: $21.95**          **ISBN: 1-55571-433-1**

This is a comprehensive guide to buying radio, television, print, direct mail, outdoor and transit advertising. It includes information on customer identification, copy writing, co-op money, interns, press releases, logo development, using the Internet, production of commercials, media sales reps, tracking records, and media forms. It takes the reader beyond, "Here's what to do," to the more important, "Here's how you do it."

**Advertising Without An Agency**                                   **Pages: 250**
**Paperback: $19.95**          **ISBN: 1-55571-429-3**

This CD-ROM nicely integrates with your version of Microsoft Office and includes; Excel templates that will compute Profit and Loss, Cash Flow, Market and Sales Forecasting; Word business templates and five example business plans; A PowerPoint presentation example; and other files, templates and business helpers that will give you a professional edge when building a business plan.

**Winning Business Plans in Color**          **Windows MS-Office Addition**
**Call for current pricing          CD-ROM**

ALL MAJOR CREDIT CARDS ACCEPTED

**CALL TO PLACE AN ORDER**
— or —
**TO RECEIVE A FREE CATALOG**          **1-800-228-2275**

*International Orders* (541) 479-9464          *Fax Orders* (541) 476-1479
*Web site* http://www.psi-research.com          *Email* sales@psi-research.com

PSI Research   P.O. Box 3727   Central Point, Oregon   97502   U.S.A.